OKiDOKi

Die Lernhilfe

**Englisch
10. Schuljahr**

Sigrid Janssen, Manfred Richter, Jochen Sperber

Schroedel Verlag GmbH

OKiDOKi
Die Lernhilfe

Englisch
10. Schuljahr

Sigrid Janssen
Manfred Richter
Jochen Sperber

Die Deutsche Bibliothek-CIP-Einheitsaufnahme
OKiDOKi: die Lernhilfe –
Hannover: Schroedel-Schulbuchverlag
Schuljahr 10. Englisch. Sigrid Janssen, Manfred Richter, Jochen Sperber – 1996
ISBN 3-507-22199-3

ISBN 3-507-22199-3

© 1996 Schroedel Schulbuchverlag GmbH, Hannover

Alle Rechte vorbehalten. Dieses Werk sowie einzelne Teile desselben sind urheberrechtlich geschützt. Jede Verwertung in anderen als den gesetzlich zugelassenen Fällen ist ohne vorherige schriftliche Zustimmung des Verlages nicht zulässig.

Layout: Jürgen Kochinke
Illustrationen: Dietmar Griese
Satz: O & S Satz GmbH, Hildesheim
Druck: Oeding, Braunschweig

Inhalt

Englisch

Kapitel 1: Zeitstufen und Zeitformen

Simple form – progressive form	5
Simple present – present progressive	7
Simple past – past progressive	11
Present perfect – simple past – present perfect progressive	16
Past perfect – past perfect progressive	23
Going to-future – will future	25
OKiDOKi?!	29

Kapitel 2: Besondere Verbformen

Infinitive – Infinitiv	31
Gerund – Gerundium	36
Participle – Partizip	40
OKiDOKi?!	44

Kapitel 3: Wichtige Satztypen

Relative clauses – Relativsätze	45
If-clauses – Bedingungssätze	50
Reported speech – Indirekte Rede	54
Passive clauses – Passivsätze	57

Kapitel 4: Wortarten

Nouns – Nomen/Substantive	61
Adverbs – Adverbien	66
Prepositions – Präpositionen	71
Conjunctions – Konjunktionen	75

Kapitel 5: Arbeit mit Texten

Teenage Tragedy	80
Dian Fossey	86
A letter to the editor	92

Hallo!

Bevor es richtig losgeht mit der Arbeit, liest du am besten diese Seite. **OKiDOKi** hat nämlich ein paar Besonderheiten, die das Üben einfach machen.

Da sind zunächst mal die **Umschlagklappen.** Damit kannst du die Lösungen, die auf jeder Seite stehen, während des Übens abdecken. Und wenn du fertig bist, klappst du den Umschlag einfach wieder zurück und vergleichst die Ergebnisse.

Du mußt also nicht erst mühsam nach den richtigen Lösungen suchen und auch niemanden fragen, sondern du kannst bequem direkt vergleichen.

Außerdem gibt es drei verschiedene **Symbole,** die dich beim Üben begleiten. Der Leuchtturm signalisiert dir, daß hier besondere Tips & Hilfen verraten werden. Die Glühbirne macht darauf aufmerksam, daß hier etwas ganz Wichtiges steht, was du dir unbedingt merken solltest. Der Koffer markiert Stellen, an denen der Stoff noch einmal übersichtlich zusammengefaßt ist.

Eins ist natürlich klar: Wer schummelt, der schadet sich nur selbst. Denn er verbringt seine Zeit mit diesem Buch, ohne daß er einen größeren Nutzen davon haben wird.

OKiDOKi wünscht viel Spaß und viel Erfolg bei der Arbeit.
Falls du Fragen oder Anregungen zu unserer Lernhilfen-Reihe hast, dann freuen wir uns über deinen Brief. Hier ist die Adresse:

OKiDOKi
Schroedel Schulbuchverlag
30517 Hannover

Kapitel 1

Zeitstufen und Zeitformen

Ein zentraler Unterschied zwischen dem Englischen und dem Deutschen besteht darin, daß es im Englischen für jede Zeitstufe (= *time*: die reale Gegenwart, Vergangenheit und Zukunft) zwei Zeitformen (= *tenses*) gibt: die einfache Form *(simple form/ordinary form)* und die Verlaufsform *(progressive form/continuous form)*.

Jake is speaking loudly.   Jake spricht (zur Zeit) laut.
Jake speaks loudly.   Jake spricht (immer) laut.

Während wir im Deutschen nicht durch die Zeitform ausdrücken können, ob jemand nur zu einem bestimmten Zeitpunkt oder immer laut spricht, ist das im Englischen durch die Verwendung der *simple* oder *progressive form* möglich.

Simple form – progressive form

Unbedingt merken:
Die meisten Verben drücken Tätigkeiten oder Vorgänge aus. Sie können in der *simple form* und in der *progressive form* stehen. Die *progressive form* beschreibt in allen Zeitformen Handlungen von vorübergehender Dauer. Sie betont den Verlauf einer Handlung, wobei Anfang und Ende der Handlung unerheblich sind.
Bei der *simple form* dagegen interessiert nicht der Verlauf. Sie wird für abgeschlossene Handlungen gebraucht.
Da die *progressive form* den Verlauf von Vorgängen beschreibt, können Verben, deren Bedeutung etwas Unveränderliches ausdrückt, nicht in der *progressive form* verwendet werden. Das sind Verben der Wahrnehmung, der Zuneigung oder Abneigung, Zustandsverben und Verben des Meinens oder Wissens.

Verben der Wahrnehmung		Verben der Zuneigung/Abneigung	
to feel	to see	to dislike	to love
to hear	to smell	to hate	to prefer
to notice	to taste	to like	to want

1 Translate using the simple present or present progressive.

Die Katze riecht das Fleisch.   Das Fleisch riecht gut.

_____

Ich probiere die Suppe.   Sie schmeckt wunderbar.

_____

Ich treffe (see) Paul am Sonntag.   Ich verstehe (see), was du meinst.

_____

Ich fühle mich gut.   Ich glaube (feel), es wird zu spät.

Lösungen

1. The cat is smelling the meat. –
The meat smells good.
I'm tasting the soup. –
It tastes wonderful.
I'm seeing Paul on Sunday. –
I see what you mean.
I'm feeling fine. –
I feel it's getting too late.

Zeitstufen und Zeitformen

Zustandsverben	Verben des Meinens oder Wissens
to be	to agree
to belong to	to believe
to consist of	to feel
to cost	to know
to have (got)	to realize
to look	to recognize
to mean	to remember
to need	to see
to seem	to suppose
to smell (of)	to think
to sound	to understand
to taste (of)	to wonder

1 Translate using the simple present or present progressive.

Sie sieht ihren Bruder an.

Sie sieht jung aus.

Der Arzt wiegt das Baby.

Der Rucksack wiegt 10 kg.

Er denkt an seinen Freund.

Ich glaube (think), du hast recht.

Ich frühstücke.

Er hat kurze Haare.

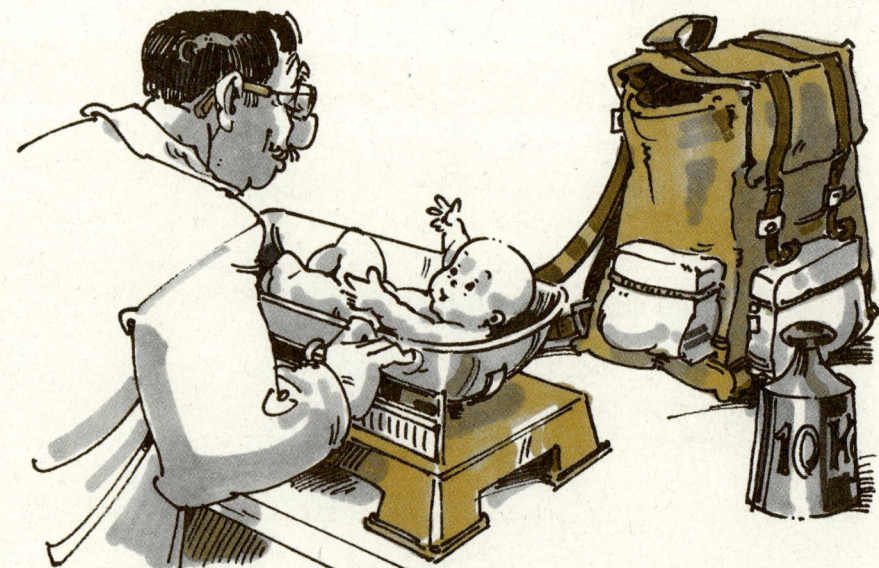

Lösungen

1. She's looking at her brother. –
   She looks young.
   The doctor is weighing the baby. –
   The rucksack weighs 10 kilos.
   He's thinking of his friend. –
   I think you're right.
   I'm having breakfast. –
   He has short hair.

Zeitstufen und Zeitformen

Seite 7

Simple present – present progressive

Unbedingt merken:
Das *simple present* drückt aus, daß etwas regelmäßig oder gewohnheitsmäßig geschieht.
Wenn sich etwas immer, niemals, häufig, manchmal oder normalerweise ereignet, steht das *simple present*. Es beschreibt damit auch unabänderliche Zustände, Gesetzmäßigkeiten oder Tatsachen, z. B. Hobby, Beruf oder Fähigkeiten.

He works in York.	Der ständige Arbeitsplatz ist York.
Many people believe in horoscopes.	Viele glauben an Horoskope.
Necessity is the mother of invention.	Not macht – immer – erfinderisch.

1 Translate into English.

Normalerweise bekommen wir die Zeitung um 7 Uhr.

Manchmal schneit es im Frühling.

Was machst du an Wochenenden?

Sie spielt jeden Samstag Tennis.

Die Sonne geht im Osten auf.

Ich mag keinen Fisch.

Tips & Hilfen:
Es gibt Signalwörter für das *simple present*. Wenn sie in einem Satz auftauchen, dann ist die Wahrscheinlichkeit, daß du diese Zeitform verwenden mußt, ziemlich groß. Dazu gehören
- Adverbien der Häufigkeit:
  usually, generally, sometimes, normally, never, seldom, often, always, …
- Adverbien der Zeit:
  every day / month / year …   on Monday / Tuesday …
  during the holidays / week …   at Christmas / New Year / Easter …

Bei Signalwörtern ist allerdings Vorsicht geboten. *Never* gilt beispielsweise als Signalwort für das *simple present*. Du findest *never* aber auch bei anderen Zeitformen. Verlasse dich also nicht blindlings auf Signalwörter, sondern erschließe die Zeitform aus Inhalt und Zusammenhang.

Lösungen

1. We normally get the newspaper at 7 o'clock.
   It sometimes snows in spring.
   What do you do at the weekends?
   She plays tennis every Saturday.
   The sun rises in the east.
   I don't like fish.

Zeitstufen und Zeitformen

> **Unbedingt merken:**
> Das *present progressive* beschreibt die „wahre" Gegenwart, das Jetzt. Es drückt aus, daß etwas im Moment des Sprechens oder Schreibens im Verlauf ist. Es kann
> - gerade im Moment vor sich gehen:
>   Tom can't come to the phone. He is playing tennis at the moment.
> - eine vorübergehende Handlung sein, die noch nicht abgeschlossen ist:
>   Sue is reading a book on China.
>
> Während Tom tatsächlich im Moment Tennis spielt, muß Sue nicht unbedingt gerade jetzt dasitzen und das Buch lesen. Ausschlaggebend ist, daß sie sich zur Zeit mit dem Buch beschäftigt und es irgendwann durchgelesen haben wird.

> **Tips & Hilfen:**
> Es gibt nur wenige Signalwörter für das *present progressive*:
> at the moment, at present, now.
> Diese Signalwörter kommen relativ selten vor; aber das macht nichts. Setze sie probeweise ein: Paßt eins der Signalwörter, dann wähle grundsätzlich das *present progressive*.

1 Present progressive or simple present?

Sie mag Kaffee:	She _____ coffee all day long.	drink
Es riecht nach Kaffee:	She _____ coffee in the kitchen.	make
Sie sitzt am Tisch:	Pat _____ a letter.	write
Er ist Schriftsteller:	My neighbour _____ novels.	write
Der Fernseher ist an:	He _____ the football match.	watch
Sonntags im Stadion:	He _____ the match every Sunday.	watch
Das ist ihre Natur:	Chimpanzees _____ trees.	climb
Beobachtung:	Look! Julia _____ up a tree.	climb
Sicherer Arbeitsplatz:	He _____ in an insurance company.	work
Anfall von Arbeitswut:	Don't disturb him now. He _____ .	work
Sie hat Schmerzen:	Her leg _____ .	hurt
Er sitzt in der Wanne:	He _____ a bath.	have
Das Flugzeug startet:	The plane _____ .	take off
Feststellung:	Planes only _____ once.	crash
Er ist Milchtrinker:	He _____ milk.	like
Die 5. Cola!:	She _____ her fifth coke.	drink

Lösungen

1. drinks, is making, is writing, writes, is watching, watches, climb, is climbing, works, is working, hurts/is hurting, is having, is taking off, crash, likes, is drinking

Zeitstufen und Zeitformen **Seite 9**

> **Unbedingt merken:**
> Das *present progressive* wird verwendet, um Pläne für die Zukunft oder Ereignisse in der Zukunft auszudrücken. Daß es um Zukünftiges geht, muß durch eine Zeitangabe oder aus dem Zusammenhang deutlich werden.
> „Where are you going next weekend?" – „We're going to Berlin. We are staying with some friends there."

1 Put in the verbs in the simple present or present progressive.

Flights from Frankfurt to London _____ (take) 1.5 hours.

On my way to school I usually _____ (meet) many friends who _____ (go) to work.

I _____ (fly) to Greece next week.

Jim _____ (jump) very high but he _____ (not run) fast.

I can _____ (see) you _____ (wear) your best dress. _____ (you / go) to a party?

What music _____ (you / listen to) when you _____ (go) on holiday? – I _____ (listen to) classical music, but right now I _____ (listen to) acid jazz.

Look, a man _____ (running) after the train. He _____ (want) to catch it.

Can you _____ (see) anything? – I _____ (try) hard, but _____ (not / see) anything.

What _____ (you / do) next weekend?

The bus _____ (leave) in about an hour.

Lösungen

1. take;
   meet, are going;
   am flying;
   jumps, does not run;
   see, are wearing,
   Are you going;
   do you listen to, go, listen to,
   am listening to;
   is running, wants;
   see, am trying, don't see;
   are you doing;
   is leaving

Zeitstufen und Zeitformen

1 Simple present or present progressive?

Kevin sees Brian who wants to leave the house and says: Where _____ (you / go), Brian?

Brian: I _____ (go) to buy some chocolate. _____ (you / want) anything from the shops?

Kevin: No, thanks. You always _____ (eat) chocolate, don't you, Brian?

How many bars _____ (you / buy) a day?

Brian: I _____ (not eat) very many – perhaps two.

Sarah _____ (eat) far more than I _____ (do). She _____ (spend) £6 a week on chocolate.

Mrs Benson: My son never _____ (write) to me. So I never _____ (know) how he _____ (be).

_____ your daughter _____ (write) to you, Mrs Black?

Mrs Black: Yes, she _____ (write) a letter every week.

She _____ (seem) to like writing letters. She _____ (write) about the things she _____ (do) and _____ (tell) me how she _____ (be).

Steve and Mick are on the train. Steve says: I usually _____ (go) by train but today I _____ (go) by bus.

It _____ (take) longer but it _____ (cost) less.

Mick _____ (sit) next to me and he _____ (read) an old newspaper.

He _____ (not like) the bus at all, so he usually _____ (take) the train.

Every Friday he _____ (leave) work at 4 o'clock and _____ (walk) to the train station.

Lösungen

1. are you going, am going, Do you want, eat, do you buy, don't eat, eats, do, spends

   writes, know, is, Does your daughter write, writes, seems, writes, does, tells, is

   go, am going, takes, costs, is sitting, is reading, does not like, takes, leaves, walks

Zusammenfassung:
Simple present steht für gewohnheitsmäßige Handlungen und allgemeingültige Tatsachen.
Present progressive steht für Geschehen in der realen Gegenwart (Jetzt) und für Geschehen in der Zukunft.

Zeitstufen und Zeitformen

Simple past – past progressive

Unbedingt merken:
Im Deutschen gibt es keinen Bedeutungsunterschied zwischen den folgenden Sätzen:
Jch war gestern im Zoo. (Präteritum)
Jch bin gestern im Zoo gewesen. (Perfekt)
Im Englischen wird streng zwischen *simple past* und *present perfect* unterschieden. Der Besuch im Zoo ist vergangen und vorbei. Er hat nichts mehr mit der Gegenwart zu tun. Daher kann nur das *simple past* stehen:
J <u>was</u> at the zoo yesterday.

Tips & Hilfen:
Hüte dich bei Übersetzungen ins Englische vor einer einfachen Gleichsetzung deutscher und englischer Zeitformen.

Wo hast du das Ticket gekauft?   muß so übersetzt werden:
Where did you buy the ticket?   Und nicht etwa:
Where have you bought the ticket?

1 Translate into English.

Gestern habe ich meinen Bruder im Krankenhaus besucht.

___

Lynette traf Andy letzte Woche.

___

Ostern war ich in England.

___

Nach dem Unfall hat mein Vater ein neues Auto gekauft.

___

Bert kaufte eine Zeitung und wartete auf den Bus.

___

Hast du Oasis in der Talkshow gesehen?

___

Unbedingt merken:
Das *simple past* wird verwendet, um deutlich zu machen, daß sich etwas zu einem bestimmten Zeitpunkt in der Vergangenheit oder in einem in der Vergangenheit abgeschlossenen Zeitraum ereignete und keinen Bezug zur Gegenwart hat. Das gilt besonders, wenn mehrere Ereignisse aufeinander folgen.

Lösungen

1. Yesterday I visited my brother in hospital.
   Lynette met Andy last week.
   I was in England at Easter.
   After the accident my father bought a new car.
   Bert bought a newspaper and waited for the bus.
   Did you see Oasis in the talkshow?

Zeitstufen und Zeitformen

>
> **Tips & Hilfen:**
> Zeitpunkt oder Zeitraum einer Handlung können angegeben sein oder gehen aus dem Zusammenhang hervor:
> Did you see Michael Jackson on TV last night?
> That's a nice cap you're wearing. Where did you buy it?
> Da ich die Mütze sehe, muß sie vorher (in der Vergangenheit) gekauft worden sein.
> **Signalwörter für das *simple past*:**
> then (damals), yesterday (gestern), at that time / moment (zu jener Zeit), in 1989 (im Jahr 1989), between 1969 and 1978 (zwischen 1969 und 1978), long ago (vor langer Zeit), last week / year ... (letzte Woche, ...), an hour / two days / a week ago ... (vor einer Stunde, ...)

Wenn besonders betont werden soll, daß etwas, was einmal war, heute nicht mehr oder anders ist, verwendet man *used to* + Infinitiv.

> I used to visit him every week when I first got to London.
> = Jetzt besuche ich ihn nicht mehr jede Woche.
> I never used to drive slowly. But now I do.
> = Im Gegensatz zu früher fahre ich heute langsamer.

1 Translate into English using *used to*.

Vor zwei Jahren bin ich ziemlich oft nach England geflogen.

_____

Früher hat Ron mich oft besucht.

_____

Früher habe ich viel gelesen.

_____

Vor ein paar Jahren kam Robert immer mit dem Fahrrad.

_____

Früher mochte ich Milch.

_____

Lösungen

1. Two years ago I used to fly to England quite often.
   Ron used to visit me a lot.
   I used to read a lot.
   A few years ago Robert used to come by bike.
   I formerly used to like milk.

Zeitstufen und Zeitformen

> **Unbedingt merken:**
> Das *present progressive* wird für etwas verwendet, das sich im Moment des Sprechens ereignet. Überträgt man diese Regel in die Vergangenheit, hat man die Grundregel für das *past progressive*:
> Das *past progressive* drückt aus, daß eine Handlung zu einem bestimmten Zeitpunkt in der Vergangenheit im Verlauf war, also gerade vor sich ging. Anfang und Ende sind dabei unerheblich.
> At 10 o'clock Joan was watching the news.
> At that time I was beginning to get tired.

1 Translate into English using the past progressive.

Als Richard kam, gingen die anderen Gäste gerade.

_____

Um 10 Uhr schlief Karen schon.

_____

Zu der Zeit kaufte ich gerade ein.

_____

Als David anrief, machte Cathryn gerade ihre Hausaufgaben.

_____

In diesem Moment verließ Jean den Raum.

_____

Ich verließ gerade das Haus, als es zu regnen anfing.

_____

> When I walked in, the dog was barking.
>
> → was barking → was still barking → and was still barking
>   when I walked in
>
> Ein Vorgang *(the dog was barking)* ereignet sich in der Vergangenheit, und ein anderer setzt plötzlich ein *(I walked in)*. Die erste Handlung bildet praktisch den Hintergrund für die zweite und muß deshalb im *past progressive* stehen.
>
> When I walked in, the dog barked.
>
> Stehen beide Satzteile im *simple past (I walked in – the dog barked),* dann folgen jeweils abgeschlossene Handlungen aufeinander, und der Sinn ist anders: Der Hund fing erst an zu bellen, als ich hereinkam.

Lösungen

1. When Richard arrived, the other guests were just leaving.
At 10 o'clock Karen was already sleeping.
At that time I was doing the shopping.
When David called, Cathryn was doing her homework.
At that moment Jean left the room.
I was just leaving the house when it started to rain.

Zeitstufen und Zeitformen

> **Unbedingt merken:**
> Das *past progressive* wird verwendet für eine Handlung, die gerade in dem Moment vor sich ging, als eine zweite einsetzte. Die zweite Handlung steht im *simple past*.

1 Put in the simple past or past progressive of the verbs.

When Karen _____ (arrive) I _____ (listen) to a CD.
I _____ (see) Dave when I _____ (cycle) down the street.
I _____ (walk) through Hyde Park when I _____ (see) a man who _____ (follow) me.
I _____ (meet) Carl at a language course in England. He _____ (learn) French and I _____ (learn) English. But he _____ (not be) really interested in it and _____ (spend) most of his time playing the guitar.
When I _____ (walk) in, he _____ (lie) on the sofa.
While I _____ (decide) which T-shirt to buy, someone else _____ (come) and _____ (buy) it.
What _____ (you / do) when the phone _____ (ring)?
I _____ (make) tea.
And what _____ (you / do) when you heard the phone ringing?
I _____ (go) to answer it. But when I _____ (pick up) the receiver, there _____ (be) nobody there.
Some time later the phone _____ (ring) again, and this time there _____ (be) a woman at the other end who _____ (say) she _____ (ring) to ask me a few questions.

> **Unbedingt merken:**
> Das *past progressive* wird auch für mehrere gleichzeitig ablaufende Handlungen gebraucht. Das ist oft in Erzählungen oder Berichten der Fall:
> We *were sitting* in the garden. The sun *was shining*, the birds *were singing* and the children *were playing*. Suddenly we *heard* a scream.

Lösungen

1. arrived, was listening;
   saw, was cycling;
   was walking, saw, was following;
   met, was learning, was learning, wasn't, spent;
   walked, was lying;
   was deciding, came, bought;
   were you doing, rang;
   was making;
   rang, was, said, was ringing

Zeitstufen und Zeitformen

1 Put in the verbs in the simple past or past progressive.

I remember that Wednesday when I _____ (be) new in the firm and _____ (leave) work in the afternoon to watch a football match. I _____ (enjoy) it very much as my favourite team _____ _____ (win) although their rivals _____ (do) their best not to lose. I _____ (shout) and _____ (encourage) my team when I suddenly _____ (see) a man who _____ (shout) encouragement to the other team. I _____ (recognize) him after a while. He _____ (be) our managing director. I _____ (think) he _____ (not / know) me by sight and only as a name on the payroll. But I _____ (want) to be careful. I _____ (decide) to creep away to another part of the grounds. It _____ (be) not so easy because lots of people _____ (stand) in my way. I also _____ (notice) that the managing director's glance _____ (wander) in my direction.

The following day, while I _____ (work) overtime, the managing director _____ (come) into my office. He _____ (say) hello and _____ (want) to know what I _____ (do) there at that time. I _____ (explain) that I _____ (work) late because I _____ (have) important orders to catch up with.

When he _____ (leave) the office, he suddenly _____ (stop) and _____ (say): "I hope you _____ (enjoy) Wednesday's match as much as I _____ (do)."

Zusammenfassung:
Simple past wird verwendet für in der Vergangenheit abgeschlossene Handlungen.
Past progressive wird verwendet für Handlungen, die zu einem bestimmten Zeitpunkt in der Vergangenheit im Verlauf waren.

Lösungen

1. was, left, enjoyed, was winning / won, were doing / did, was shouting, encouraging, saw, was shouting, recognized, was, thought, didn't know, wanted, decided, was, were standing, noticed, was wandering, was working, came, said, wanted, was doing, explained, was working, had, was leaving, stopped, said, enjoyed, did

Zeitstufen und Zeitformen

Present perfect – simple past – present perfect progressive

Unbedingt merken:
Das *present perfect* wird verwendet, um Auswirkungen vergangener Handlungen auf die Gegenwart zu betonen. Der Zeitpunkt der Handlung ist unwichtig. Wichtig ist nur ihre Beziehung zur Gegenwart. Das *present perfect* bildet eine Brücke zwischen Gegenwart und Vergangenheit.
Vorgänge im *present perfect* haben einen engeren Bezug zur Gegenwart als zur Vergangenheit.

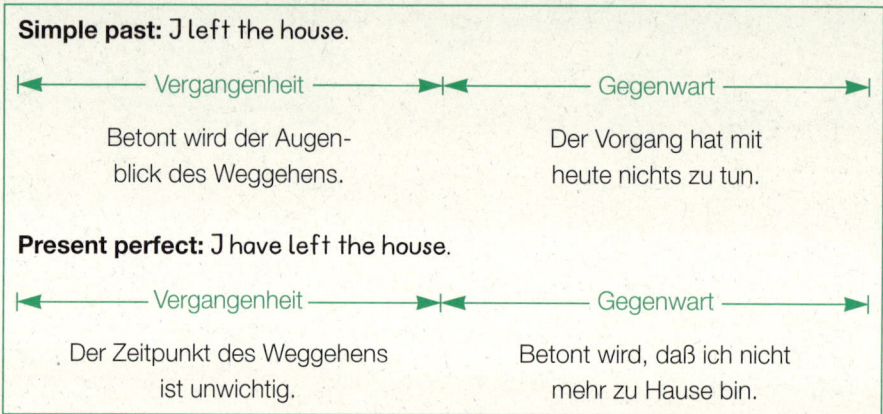

Simple past: I left the house.

◄─── Vergangenheit ───► ◄─── Gegenwart ───►

Betont wird der Augenblick des Weggehens. — Der Vorgang hat mit heute nichts zu tun.

Present perfect: I have left the house.

◄─── Vergangenheit ───► ◄─── Gegenwart ───►

Der Zeitpunkt des Weggehens ist unwichtig. — Betont wird, daß ich nicht mehr zu Hause bin.

1 Form sentences using the present perfect.

My father sold our old car last week. Our new car is blue. →
My father has bought a blue car.

Mary is at home. An hour ago she was still at the disco.

Last week my neighbour won 200,000 pounds. He drives a Ferrari now.

I met Pat at Britta's birthday last year. I don't know what she looks like now.

I wanted to do my homework last night. But I couldn't find my exercise book.

He started as a teacher in 1975. He's still a teacher at our school.

I was lucky with my fishing rod. Look, here's something for the frying-pan.

Lösungen

1. Mary has left the disco.
   My neighbour has bought a Ferrari.
   I haven't seen Pat since Britta's birthday last year.
   I haven't done my homework.
   He has been a teacher at our school since 1975.
   I have caught a fish.

Zeitstufen und Zeitformen

Unbedingt merken:
Fehlt im Satz eine genaue Zeitangabe, die angibt, wann etwas in der Vergangenheit geschehen ist, steht *present perfect*:

I've bought a new CD.   Hervorgehoben wird, daß ich jetzt eine neue CD besitze.

Wird eine Zeitbestimmung hinzugefügt, muß *simple past* stehen:

I bought a new CD yesterday.   Damit wird der Zeitpunkt des Kaufs hervorgehoben.

Nach folgenden Signalwörtern muß *present perfect* stehen:
- **yet** (bisher, schon)
- **not ... yet** (bisher noch nicht)
- **so far** (bis jetzt, bisher)
- **since** (seit, seitdem)
- **up to now** (bis heute, bis jetzt)
- **until now** (bis heute, bis jetzt)
- **all my life** (mein ganzes Leben lang)

Andere Zeitangaben, die häufig, aber nicht zwingend mit dem *present perfect* stehen, sind: *ever, never, just, always, all week, for*. Aber Vorsicht! Letztlich hängt die Zeitform von Inhalt und Zusammenhang ab!

Tips & Hilfen:
Als Folge von Handlungen kann etwas Konkretes eintreten oder eine Erfahrung, ein Wissenszuwachs:

I have lost my money. Now I can't take the bus.
I have heard the new Stones CD. It's really good.

1 Present perfect or simple past? The information at the beginning helps you to find the right tense.

Can you help me with some money? I _____ (lose) my purse.

Where's the first aid kit? I _____ (just cut) my finger with a knife.

Now the Johnsons are fighting each other. Once they _____ (be) very happy.

Mozart was a great composer. He _____ (compose) some very fine operas.

I feel better now. I _____ (have) a headache earlier today.

They haven't got any more tickets. They _____ (sell) them all.

Shakespeare lived in the 16th century. He _____ (write) a lot of plays.

Karen is not here. She _____ (go) to see a friend.

I don't know where Monica is. _____ (you / see) her?

Lösungen

1. have lost, have just cut, were, composed, had, have sold, wrote, has gone, Have you seen

Zeitstufen und Zeitformen

> **Unbedingt merken:**
> *Since* wird verwendet, wenn ein Zeitpunkt angegeben ist, an dem etwas begann, das sich bis jetzt fortsetzt:
> since 1994   since I was young
> since Friday   since we left / arrived
> *For* wird verwendet, wenn ein Zeitraum angegeben ist:
> for a few minutes   for a long time
> for five hours / a week   for ages

1 Complete the sentences with *for* and *since*.

It hasn't snowed _____ more than a week / _____ last year.
Nobody has phoned me _____ days / _____ Sunday.
I haven't been to England _____ 1993 / _____ one year.
He has lived next door _____ the last two years / _____ 1995.
I haven't been skiing _____ longer than I can remember. /
I haven't been skiing _____ I was ten.
There hasn't been a big fire here _____ years. /
There hasn't been a big fire here _____ last summer.
I'm waiting here _____ hours.
I'm waiting here _____ 10 o'clock.

2 One sentence in the simple past, the other in the present perfect. Which one?

I _____ (see) Tom yesterday.
But I _____ (not / see) him today.
He _____ (be) late all week.
Except for last Tuesday when he _____ (arrived) in time.
He _____ (not / win) many matches.
He _____ (be) much better last year.
Pat _____ (work) hard last term.
This term she _____ (be) lazy.
It _____ (be) Burt's birthday yesterday.
_____ (you / write) to him?
It _____ (snow) a lot last winter.
But it _____ (not / snow) this year.

Lösungen

1. for / since
   for / since
   since / for
   for / since
   for / since
   for / since
   for / since

2. saw / haven't seen
   has been / arrived
   hasn't won / was
   worked / has been
   was / Have you written
   snowed / hasn't snowed

Zeitstufen und Zeitformen

Seite 19

1 Present perfect or simple past? Put in the right form of the verb.

Dear Nico,

It was such a long time ago that I _____ (write) my last letter to you. As you know, we _____ (move) to San Jose a few weeks ago. My father _____ (just / find) a good job at Aspect Telecommunications.

The people here in California are pretty friendly. My mother _____ (join) a coffee club only three days after our arrival. She _____ _____ (already / make) a lot of friends. Last Saturday she _____ (throw) a party for all our neighbours. Oh, and she _____ (start) learning Spanish again.

But I don't know what it sounds like because I _____ (not / hear) her talking to anyone.

She says that she _____ (not / learn) enough yet.

School _____ (start) three weeks ago.

I _____ (choose) classes in Maths, American history, English Literature, and Chemistry. I _____ (not / get) into Photo Journalism. But they _____ (accept) me in Computer Science.

My brother _____ (freak out) several times because some kids at his school _____ (dislike) his baseball cap.

He _____ (always / be) a fan of the San Francisco 49ers, you know.

I look forward to hearing from you,

Ed

Lösungen

1. wrote, moved, has just found, joined, has already made, threw, has started, haven't heard, hasn't learnt started, have chosen (auch möglich: chose), didn't get, have accepted (auch möglich: accepted), (has) freaked out, disliked, has always been

Zeitstufen und Zeitformen

Unbedingt merken:
Im Gegensatz zum *present progressive*, das für den gegenwärtigen Augenblick gilt, wird das *present perfect progressive* (Verlaufsform) verwendet, sobald eine Beziehung zwischen Vergangenheit und Gegenwart besteht. Es steht dann, wenn von Handlungen oder Vorgängen die Rede ist, die in der Vergangenheit angefangen haben und bis in die Gegenwart hinein andauern:

I have read two newspapers this morning. →
Bis jetzt habe ich zwei Zeitungen gelesen.
I have been reading the newspaper this morning. →
Es ist immer noch vormittags, und ich lese die Zeitung immer noch.

Tips & Hilfen:
Tätigkeiten oder Vorgänge, die in der Vergangenheit begonnen haben und bis in die Gegenwart andauern, werden im Deutschen oft mit *schon* wiedergegeben. *Schon* wird nicht ins Englische übersetzt, da es bereits in der Zeitform enthalten ist:
It has been raining since yesterday.   Es regnet (schon) seit gestern.

1 Translate these sentences.

Wir sehen schon seit einer Stunde fern.
_____

Wir sitzen schon seit 9 Uhr hier.
_____

Er versucht seit Jahren, richtig Klavier zu spielen.
_____

Sie lebt schon seit vier Jahren in England.
_____

Wie lange wohnst du schon hier?
_____

Es regnet seit vier Stunden.
_____

Ich lerne seit 5 Jahren Englisch.
_____

Wie lange hast Du schon gewartet?
_____

Lösungen

1. We have been watching TV for an (oder: one) hour.
   We have been sitting here since 9 o'clock.
   He has been trying for years to play the piano properly.
   She has been living in England for four years.
   How long have you been living / have you lived here?
   It has been raining for four hours.
   I have been learning English for five years.
   How long have you been waiting?

Zeitstufen und Zeitformen *Seite 21*

 Look at the pictures. What have these people been doing or what has been happening?

English lesson

_____ for three years.

At the doctor's

_____ since 9.30.

Rain

_____ for two hours.

Shopping

_____ since 10.15.

Playing the trumpet

_____ since he was nine.

In bed

_____ all day.

Lösungen

1. They've been learning English for 3 years.
   She's been sitting / waiting at the doctor's since 9.30.
   It's been raining for two hours.
   They have been shopping since 10.15.
   He's been playing the trumpet since he was nine.
   She's been lying in bed all day.
   Auch andere Sätze sind möglich, aber die Zeitform muß entsprechend sein.

Zeitstufen und Zeitformen

1 Use the present perfect, present perfect progressive, or simple past.

Dear Laura,

It was five months ago that I _____ (promise) to write you a long letter. Well, here it is. I _____ (not / forget) you. It's just that I _____ (work) very hard for school for some months.

Well, I _____ (get) some news for you. I hope you remember our English teacher. For years we _____ (tell) him strange stories, which he _____ (always / listen to).

It's incredible! He _____ (never / find) out that we _____ (tell) him stories without any truth in them.

Only yesterday one of my classmates _____ (have) him on. In a sweet voice she _____ (say):

"Sir, I _____ (wait) here for fifteen minutes. But Julia _____ (not / turn) up yet."

You should have seen our teacher. Off he _____ (storm)! When he had disappeared, Julia _____ (come) round the corner. After twenty minutes our teacher _____ (be) back again, breathing heavily. When he _____ (see) Julia he _____ (say) with a big smile on his face: "I'm so happy that you _____ (find) your way back again."

Unbelievable, isn't it? Well, I _____ (write) enough for today. I look forward to hearing from you soon.

Yours,
Sarah

Lösungen

1. I promised
   I haven't forgotten
   I've been working
   I've got
   we've been telling
   he's always listened to
   He's never found out
   we told
   had him on
   she said
   I've been waiting
   Julia hasn't turned up
   he stormed
   Julia came
   our teacher was
   he saw
   he said
   you've found
   I've written

Zusammenfassung:
Das *present perfect* steht für zeitlich nicht näher bestimmte Vorgänge der Vergangenheit, deren Folgen bis in die Gegenwart reichen.
Das *present perfect progressive* steht für Vorgänge, die in der Vergangenheit beginnen und bis in die Gegenwart reichen.

Zeitstufen und Zeitformen

Past perfect – past perfect progressive

 Unbedingt merken:
Das *past perfect* wird für Handlungen verwendet, die vor einem bestimmten Zeitpunkt in der Vergangenheit abgeschlossen wurden:
Robert didn't come because he had broken his leg.
Das *past perfect progressive* wird für Handlungen verwendet, die bis zu einem bestimmten Zeitpunkt in der Vergangenheit andauerten:
When Stewart finally arrived J had been waiting for half an hour.

At nine o'clock last Saturday J had been waiting for two hours, but no guests had arrived.

|—————————|—▶| X |——▶| JETZT |

for two hours · at 9 o'clock last Saturday

andauernder Vorgang in der Vergangenheit · Zeitpunkt in der Vergangenheit · aktueller Zeitpunkt, an dem die Aussage gemacht wird

Past perfect und *past perfect progressive* erlauben eine Rückschau von einem Zeitpunkt in der Vergangenheit aus.

1 Past perfect or past perfect progressive? Is it about finished or continuing actions in the past?

I couldn't go into the garden. It _____ (rain) for hours and hours.

She lost her fur gloves. They _____ (cost) a lot of money.

When it started to rain, she _____ (wait) for two hours.

Not a piece of cake was left over. The guests _____ (eat) everything.

After two hours I noticed that I _____ (go) to the wrong restaurant.

The two boys were dirty. They _____ (play) football for two hours.

They were extremely tired. They _____ (travel) for 16 hours.

When we got to the station, the train _____ (just / leave).

I wasn't hungry because we _____ (have) supper one hour before.

I thought that I _____ (send) you the cheque a week before.

Monica wondered who _____ (leave) the door open.

When the police arrived, the thieves _____ (run) away.

Lösungen

1. had been raining
 had cost
 had been waiting
 had eaten
 had gone
 had been playing
 had been travelling
 had just left
 had had
 had sent
 had left
 had run

Zeitstufen und Zeitformen

When we arrived, they **had stopped** their work.

When we arrived, they **stopped** their work.

Sie hatten schon mit ihrer Arbeit aufgehört, **bevor** wir kamen.

Sie hörten erst **nach** unserer Ankunft auf zu arbeiten.

1 Past perfect or past perfect progressive?

Last Monday my wife told me that she _____ (see) something terrible. She _____ (watch) a man for some time who _____ (stand) on a window-sill for several hours trying to put an end to his life.

The following day we read in the newspaper what _____ (happen). The man _____ (lose) his wife in a car accident after they _____ (live) together for nearly 26 years. They _____ (dream) of a sailing trip to the Carribean. When the accident happened they _____ (already / buy) the boat.

Lösungen

1. had seen
   had been watching
   had been standing
   had happened
   had lost
   had been living
   had been dreaming
   had already bought

Zusammenfassung:

Das *past perfect* wird verwendet, wenn eine Handlung vor einem bestimmten Zeitpunkt in der Vergangenheit stattgefunden hat.

Das *past perfect progressive* wird verwendet, wenn eine Handlung bis zu einem bestimmten Zeitpunkt in der Vergangenheit andauerte.

Zeitstufen und Zeitformen

Going to-future – will-future

Unbedingt merken:
Im Englischen gibt es verschiedene Möglichkeiten, Zukünftiges auszudrücken. Eine Möglichkeit ist das *going to-future*.
Das *going to-future* wird verwendet, um auszudrücken,
- daß wir die feste Absicht haben, etwas in Zukunft zu tun. Wichtig ist, daß der Entschluß feststeht.
I'm going to work harder.
Ich beabsichtige / ich habe fest vor, etwas zu tun (Absicht).
- daß ein Ereignis mit Sicherheit oder großer Wahrscheinlichkeit in naher Zukunft eintreten wird. Meistens gibt es dafür schon Anzeichen:
It's going to rain.
Finstere Wolken ziehen auf. Alles deutet darauf hin, daß es in Kürze regnen wird (große Wahrscheinlichkeit).

Tips & Hilfen:
Das *going to-future* kann nicht beliebig angewendet werden. Ein nicht erfüllbarer Wunsch ist zum Beispiel keine feste Absicht.
Wunsch: I want to leave soon.
Ich kann aber nicht, weil Peter mich nicht läßt.
Absicht: I'm going to leave soon.
Obwohl Peter nicht möchte, daß ich gehe, werde ich es tun.

1 Translate using the going to-future.

Ich werde nächste Woche meinen Geburtstag feiern.

_____ A W

Sie kriegt zum Geburtstag ein Fahrrad.

_____ A W

Sharon fliegt Sonntag nach London.

_____ A W

Karen hat mir gesagt, daß sie nächstes Jahr heiratet.

_____ A W

Sieh dir den Himmel an. Es wird bald schneien.

_____ A W

Die Tür ist offen. Der Vogel wird gleich wegfliegen.

_____ A W

2 Kreuze jeweils an, ob eine Absicht (A) oder eine Wahrscheinlichkeit (W) vorliegt.

Lösungen

1. und 2.
I'm going to celebrate
my birthday next week. A
She's going to get a bike
for her birthday. A
Sharon's going to fly
to London on Sunday. A
Karen told me that she's
going to marry next year. A
Look at the sky. It's going
to snow soon. W
The door is open.
The bird is going to fly
away in a minute. W

Seite 26 *Zeitstufen und Zeitformen*

> **Unbedingt merken:**
> Das *will-future* wird verwendet, um zukünftige Ereignisse oder Zustände zu beschreiben, die nicht von Willen oder Absicht des Sprechers beeinflußt werden können. Sie sind von äußeren Bedingungen abhängig, so daß nur Vermutungen angestellt werden können:
> *I bet it'll rain tomorrow.*
> Außerdem kann man mit dem *will-future* spontane Entscheidungen zum Ausdruck zu bringen. Dabei ist es unerheblich, ob sie ernst gemeint sind oder nicht. Oft wird damit aber ein Versprechen oder eine Drohung ausgedrückt:
> *The weather is so bad! I'll fly to Mallorca tomorrow!*

1 Fill in the *will-future* of the verbs in brackets.

I _____ (know) the result of the election by tomorrow. **V E**
I think prices _____ (rise). **V E**
I can't reach the cup. – I _____ (get) it for you. **V E**
You _____ (understand) it when you see it. **V E**
It _____ (be) dark soon. **V E**
If you don't hurry you _____ (miss) the train. **V E**
Richard's in trouble? I _____ (help) him. **V E**
Oh dear, it's late. I _____ (sleep) all day tomorrow. **V E**
I guess he _____ (be) back at 10.30. **V E**
I haven't seen Ron for ages. I _____ (call) him now. **V E**
_____ (you / have) time to see him this afternoon? **V E**
I hope you _____ (pass) the exam. **V E**
If you learn English you _____ (get) a good job. **V E**
I'm sure you _____ (like) my new CD. **V E**
You _____ (feel) better when you've had something to eat. **V E**

2 In welchen Sätzen wird ein nicht beeinflußbares Ereignis bzw. eine Vermutung (V), in welchen ein spontaner Entschluß (E) ausgedrückt?

> **Tips & Hilfen:**
> Die Wörter *to hope, to think, to believe, to promise, to guess, to suppose, to assume, perhaps, possibly, probably, maybe* sind Signalwörter und deuten auf die Verwendung des *will-futures* hin, denn sie drücken eine Meinung, Hoffnung oder Wahrscheinlichkeit aus.

Lösungen

1. und 2.
will know	V
will rise	V
will get	E
will understand	V
will be	V
will miss	V
will help	E
will sleep	E oder V
will be	V
will call	E
Will you have	V
will pass	V
will get	V
will like	V
will feel	V

Zeitstufen und Zeitformen

1 *Will-future* or *going to-future*?

Wie lange wird es dauern?
_____

Ich rufe dich heute nachmittag an.
_____

Sie wird die Antwort wissen.
_____

Ich werde sie morgen sehen.
_____

Ich werde nicht vergessen, morgen zu kommen.
_____

Wenn du die Flasche fallen läßt, zerbricht sie.
_____

Ich glaube es erst, wenn ich es sehe.
_____

Glaubst du, er erkennt mich noch?
_____

Da es schon den ganzen Tag regnet, findet das Spiel nicht statt.
_____

2 Put in the *will-future* or *going to-future*.

Absicht:	J _____	see my grandma next Saturday.
Vermutung:	He _____	win the tennis match.
Versprechen:	J _____	give you the money next week.
Absicht:	J _____	be a journalist.
Drohung:	J _____	kill you.
Entscheidung:	J think J _____	go to bed now.
Wahrscheinlichkeit:	They are the better team. They _____ win.

Tips & Hilfen:
In bestimmten Fällen ist sowohl *will-future* als auch *going to-future* richtig. Im Zweifelsfall – wenn der Kontext nicht eindeutig ist – verwende *will*.

Seite 27

Lösungen

1. How long will it take?
   I will / I'm going to call you this afternoon.
   She'll know the answer.
   I'll / I'm going to see her tomorrow.
   I won't forget to come tomorrow.
   If you drop the bottle it'll break.
   I'll believe it when I see it.
   Do you think he'll recognize me?
   As it has been raining all day the match will not take place.

2. am going to, will, will am going to, will, will, will

Zeitstufen und Zeitformen

1 *Will-future* or *going to-future*?

No, I can't go swimming with you.

_____ do my homework.

Mr Stewart thinks it _____ snow soon.

Why did you throw these shoes away? –

I _____ buy some new ones tomorrow.

She _____ have a baby in June.

She _____ have a baby one day.

It's almost 7 o'clock. I _____ watch the news on TV.

It looks as if the weather _____ change.

I'm pretty sure she _____ call.

I didn't buy any chocolate because I _____ stop eating sweets.

What ___you___ do when you leave school?

Zusammenfassung:
Das *will-future* wird verwendet, wenn von künftigen Ereignissen und Zuständen die Rede ist, die der Sprecher nicht beeinflussen kann, oder wenn ein spontaner Entschluß gefaßt wird, etwas sofort oder künftig zu tun. Das *going to-future* wird verwendet, wenn ausgedrückt werden soll, was man in der Zukunft zu tun beabsichtigt, oder wenn ein Ereignis mit Sicherheit oder großer Wahrscheinlichkeit eintreten wird.

Unbedingt merken:
Die englischen tenses sind keine ganz einfache Sache. Wenn du aber ein paar wichtige Regeln auswendig lernst, wirst du viel besser und leichter mit ihnen zurechtkommen.
- *Simple present* für Tatsachen und gewohnheitsmäßige Handlungen.
- *Present progressive* für im Verlauf befindliche Handlungen der Gegenwart.
- *Present perfect* für Handlungen, deren Folgen in die Gegenwart reichen.
- *Present perfect progressive* für Handlungen, die bis in die Gegenwart andauern.
- *Simple past* für abgeschlossene Handlungen der Vergangenheit ohne Bezug zur Gegenwart.
- *Past progressive* für im Verlauf befindliche Handlungen der Vergangenheit.
- *Past perfect* für Vorvergangenheit.
- *Will-future* für künftige Ereignisse, die sich nicht beeinflussen lassen.
- *Going to-future* für beabsichtigtes Handeln in der Zukunft.

Lösungen

1. I'm going to do
   it will snow
   I'm going to buy
   She's going to have
   She will have
   I'm going to watch
   is going to change
   she will call
   I'm going to stop
   are you going to do

Zeitstufen und Zeitformen

Seite 29

OKiDOKi?!

- Fill in the simple present, present perfect, simple past, past progressive or past perfect.

Something _____ (jingle) in my head when I _____ (have) fish for lunch. I _____ (know) that a friend of mine _____ (say) something about fish and bells. In the evening I _____ (ring) him up and _____ (ask) him.

"That's nothing special," he said. "Yesterday I _____ (go) fishing and _____ (not / go) home before a fish _____ (ring) the bell."

I _____ (never / hear) such a strange thing before.

"Just let me get it straight", I _____ (say). "The fish _____ (ring) the bell and _____ (tell) you that it _____ (want) to go home with you."

"Exactly! You _____ (get) it. You know, I _____ (fix) the bell to the fishing rod. You always do that when its dark. When the bell rings, you know that a fish _____ (eat) the worm. That's how you catch fish at night."

He told me that he _____ (buy) the bells in a shop.

Something _____ (go) on in my brain again. _____ (not / be) this a nice present for my daughter, who is 16? The following day I _____ (buy) four bells and _____ (take) them home. With a smile on my face I told my daughter that I _____ (buy) something for her.

"I _____ (get) something special for you", I said.

She _____ (open) the small parcel and _____ (look) inside.

"_____ (you / want) to go fishing with me at night?" she suddenly _____ (ask)

Lösungen

- jingled / was jingling, had / was having, knew, had said, rang, asked, went, didn't go, had rung, had never heard, said, rang, told, wanted, have got, fixed, has eaten, had bought, was going, Wasn't, bought, took, had bought, have got, opened, looked
Do you want, asked

Zeitstufen und Zeitformen

Seite 30

⚀ Fill in the present perfect, simple past, past progressive or past perfect.

Most people know what an ear clip is but _____ (you / ever / hear) of a shoe clip? Yesterday I _____ (meet) a young girl in the office who _____ (wear) a bell as a shoe clip. She _____ (fix) it to her shoe somehow. Whenever she _____ (open) the door and _____ (go) to her seat, the bell _____ (jingle) to the amusement of the others.

I _____ (ask) her where she _____ (buy) the bell, but she only _____ (smile) and _____ (say): "A friend _____ (give) me the bell as a present."

Lösungen

⚀ have you ever heard
　met
　was wearing
　had fixed
　opened
　went
　jingled
　asked
　had bought
　smiled
　said
　gave

Kapitel 2
Besondere Verbformen

Von allen Verben gibt es außer den Personalformen, die in verschiedenen Zeitstufen gebraucht werden können, auch sogenannte infinite (nicht auf eine Person / eine Zeit festgelegte) Formen. Dazu gehören der Infinitiv, die Partizipien und das Gerundium.

Der Gebrauch dieser Formen ist jeweils mit einer bestimmten Aussageabsicht verbunden. Anders als im Deutschen ist die Verwendung zum Teil auch davon abhängig, mit welchen anderen Verben die betreffende infinite Form jeweils verbunden ist.

Infinitive – Infinitiv

 Unbedingt merken:
Alle Vollverben haben einen Infinitiv. In Sätzen kann ein Infinitiv mit *to (infinitive with to)* oder ohne *to (infinitive without to)* stehen:
I want to drink some milk. But I can't find any.
Der Infinitiv mit *to* steht – wie im Deutschen – nach Adjektiven (besonders in Verbindung mit *too* oder *enough*):
It's not easy to get good marks.   It's too cold to go for a walk.
He's good enough to win.
Für die Verneinung wird *not* vor den Infinitiv gesetzt:
The sign said not to walk on the grass.

1 Translate into English.

Mein Onkel hat beschlossen, sein Geschäft zu verkaufen.

Er weigerte sich, für sechs Monate nach Dubai zu gehen.

Wir entschieden uns, nicht auszugehen, weil das Wetter so schlecht war.

Er versprach, nicht noch einmal zu spät zu kommen.

Wie alt warst du, als du gelernt hast, Fahrrad zu fahren?

Wir können es uns nicht leisten, wieder nach Kalifornien zu fliegen.

Er rechnete damit (expect), sein Englisch zu verbessern (improve).

Lösungen

1. My uncle has decided to sell his business.
He refused to go to Dubai for six months.
We decided not to go out because the weather was so bad.
He promised not to be late again.
How old were you when you learned to ride a bicycle?
We can't afford to fly to California again.
He expected to improve his English.

Besondere Verbformen

> **Unbedingt merken:**
> Nach bestimmten Verben steht immer der Infinitiv mit *to*.
> Infinitive mit *to* können eine Absicht ausdrücken und im Deutschen durch einen Infinitivsatz mit „(um) … zu" wiedergegeben werden:
> I learnt to speak English.   Ich habe gelernt, Englisch zu sprechen.
> I ran to catch the bus.   Ich rannte, um den Bus zu erwischen.

can afford	sich leisten können	to promise	versprechen
to agree	zustimmen	to refuse	sich weigern
to decide	sich entschließen	to seem	scheinen
to expect	erwarten, damit rechnen	to try	versuchen
to hope	hoffen	to want	(etwas tun) wollen
to learn	lernen	would like	möchte(n)
to plan	planen	would love	gern (tun)

> **Unbedingt merken:**
> Nach Verben, die ausdrücken, daß A etwas von B will, steht ein Objekt, gefolgt von einem Infinitiv mit *to*:
> Subjekt + Verb + Objekt + Infinitiv mit *to*   Subjekt + Verb + Objekt + Inf. mit *to*
> Sarah wants Tom to call her.   Sarah wants him to call her.
> Im Deutschen steht dafür oft ein Nebensatz, der mit *daß* beginnt. Im Englischen darf nach *want* und *would like / love* auf keinen Fall ein Nebensatz mit *that* stehen.

to advise	raten	to help	helfen
to allow	erlauben	to invite	einladen, auffordern
to ask	bitten	to remind	daran erinnern
to encourage	ermutigen	to teach	lehren, beibringen
to expect	erwarten, verlangen	to tell	befehlen, sagen
to force	zwingen	to want	wollen
to get	veranlassen	to warn	warnen, anraten

1 Complete the sentences based on the dialogue.

Carol: Oh, Tom! I thought you weren't going to visit me again. Why can't you leave me alone. Go home, please. – Tom: Please, Carol, let me in to use the phone. – Carol: You can use the phone. But that's all. – Tom: I promise. I won't bother you.

Carol hadn't expected Tom _____

She asked _____

Tom begged _____

Carol allowed _____

Tom promised _____

Lösungen

1. Carol hadn't expected Tom to visit her again.
   She asked him to leave her alone / to go home.
   Tom begged her to let him in to use the phone.
   Carol allowed him to use her phone.
   Tom promised not to bother her.

Besondere Verbformen

> **Unbedingt merken:**
> Infinitive mit *to* können auch statt Relativsätzen stehen. Das ist besonders nach Superlativen *(the best, …)*, nach Ordinalzahlen *(the first, the second, …)* und nach *the only (one), the next (one), the last (one)* der Fall. Die Verneinung wird mit *not* + Infinitiv gebildet.

The best singer	to take part in the competition		is English.
The best singer	who takes part in the competition		is English.
Der beste Sänger,	*der an dem Wettbewerb teilnimmt,*		*ist Engländer.*
Peter was the first	to start	and the last	to finish.
Peter was the first	who started	and the last	who finished.
Peter war der erste,	*der begann,*	*und der letzte,*	*der fertig wurde.*

1 Replace the relative pronoun by the correct infinitive.

Mr Smith was the first who noticed the fire.

Mr Smith _____

Peter was the only classmate who went to the army.

Peter _____

It's probably the best cake which we can buy.

It's _____

Sally is the only girl who expects some presents.

Sally _____

He gave her a comic which she could read on the train.

He _____

The racing car which came in last was driven by a German.

The racing car _____

Carl is the next who is going to England to study.

Carl _____

The earliest train which arrived came from Bedford.

The _____

Our teacher was the only one who did not come to the school party.

Our teacher _____

My friend Tony was the second who finished the race.

My friend Tony _____

Our dog Molly was the only one who was left at home.

Our dog Molly _____

Lösungen

1. … the first to notice …
   … only classmate to go …
   … best cake to buy.
   … only girl to expect …
   … a comic to read …
   … to come in last …
   … the next to go to …
   … the earliest train to arrive …
   … the only one not to come …
   … the second to finish …
   … the only one to be left …

Seite 33

Besondere Verbformen

Unbedingt merken:
Der Infinitiv mit *to* nach Fragewörtern wie *how, what, when, where, which, who* und nach *whether* (ob) drückt ein Können, Sollen oder Müssen aus und verkürzt den Satz.

Lynette wondered
how to get home.
how she should get home.
wie sie nach Hause kommen sollte.

who to ask.
who she can ask.
wen sie fragen kann.

We didn't know
which way to go.
which way we should go.
welchen Weg wir gehen sollten.

whether to turn left or right.
whether we should turn left or right.
ob wir nach links oder rechts abbiegen sollten.

1 Put in a question word and a matching verb.

how, what, when, whether, which, who
apply, buy, come, do, get, invite, prepare, ride, use, wear

Do you know _____ to the bus stop?

Would you know _____ if there was a fire alarm?

You'll never forget _____ a horse.

I didn't know _____ a CD or not.

She wondered _____ kind of paint _____ for her room.

I wonder _____ to my birthday party.

Have you decided _____ for the job or not?

He'll tell you _____ for the match.

I asked my father _____ home tonight.

I asked my mother _____ dress _____.

Zusammenfassung:
Der Infinitiv mit *to* steht
- nach Adjektiven, besonders in Verbindung mit *too* und *enough*;
- nach bestimmten Verben, die Absichten, Wünsche, Bitten, Befehle ausdrücken;
- nach bestimmten Verben + Objekt;
- zur Verkürzung von Relativsätzen und nach Fragewörtern.

Lösungen

1. how to get, what to do, how to ride, whether to buy, what kind of paint to use, who to invite, whether to apply, how to prepare, when to come, which dress to wear

Besondere Verbformen

Seite 35

Unbedingt merken:
Neben dem Infinitiv mit *to* gibt es auch den Infinitiv ohne *to*. Der Infinitiv ohne *to* steht nach den Hilfsverben *can / could, may / might, must / needn't, shall / should* und *will / would* und nach *do /does / did*.

You can go if you like.   You may visit him.
You will contact her.   You didn't call her.

Tips & Hilfen:
Nach *to feel* = fühlen, *to let* = (zu)lassen, erlauben und *to make* = (veran)lassen, zwingen, *to see* = sehen, *to watch* = zuschauen, beobachten kann auch ein Objekt mit einem Infinitiv ohne *to* stehen:

Subjekt	Verb	Objekt	Infinitiv +	Objekt
Ed	lets	Peter	ride	his bike.
Sam and Rick	make	their little brother	clean	their bikes.

1 Translate these sentences.

Ich zwang (make) ihn, mir mein Geld zurückzugeben.

___

Sie läßt es zu (let), daß ihre Kinder sehr lange aufbleiben.

___

Wir schauten unserer Mannschaft beim Fußballspielen zu.

___

Ich sah den Jungen um die Ecke verschwinden.

___

Ich fühlte etwas meinen Arm heraufkrabbeln.

___

Ich möchte, daß Ihre Kinder ruhig sind.

___

Paula brachte ihn dazu (make), höflich zu reden.

___

Alles, was ich tat, war, ihn anzusehen.

___

Lösungen

1. I made him give me back my money.
She lets her children stay up very late.
We watched our team play football.
I saw the boy disappear round the corner.
I felt something crawl up my arm.
I want your children to be quiet.
Paula made him talk politely.
All I did was look at him.

Gerund – Gerundium

 Unbedingt merken:
Das Gerundium ist eine grammatische Form, die es im Deutschen nicht gibt. Sie entspricht in etwa dem substantivierten Infinitiv *(smoking – das Rauchen)*, kann aber auch durch einen Nebensatz übersetzt werden. Das Gerundium wird durch Anhängen von *-ing* an den Infinitiv gebildet. Es hat einerseits Eigenschaften des Verbs, wird aber andererseits wie ein Substantiv verwendet.

Das Gerundium kann – wie ein Verb – ein Objekt haben:
Smoking is bad for you.   (= Gerundium)
Smoking cigarettes is bad for you.   (= Gerundium + Objekt)

Das Gerundium kann – wie ein Substantiv – Subjekt oder Objekt sein:
Smoking is not healthy.   *Rauchen ist nicht gesund.*
J don't mind walking.   *Ich habe nichts dagegen zu laufen.*

Nach manchen Verben muß das Gerundium stehen.
Patty kept on walking.   Niemals: *Patty kept on to walk.*

Aber: Nach *would like / love* darf kein Gerundium stehen, sondern nur der Infinitiv:
J'd love to go to London.   Niemals: *J'd love going to London.*
Would you like to go, too?   *Would you like going, too?*

Verben, nach denen immer das Gerundium steht:

to avoid	(ver)meiden	to keep (on)	weiter(machen)
to consider	in Betracht ziehen	to mind	etwas dagegen haben
to deny	abstreiten	to practice	üben
to dislike	ungern tun/nicht mögen	to risk	wagen, riskieren
to enjoy	gern tun, genießen	to stop	aufhören (mit)
to finish	aufhören (mit)	to suggest	vorschlagen

1 Translate these sentences using the gerund.

Tennis spielen ist ihr Lieblingshobby (favourite hobby).

Er riskierte es, sein Leben zu verlieren.

Sie hörte auf zu rauchen und zu trinken.

Carl vermied es, meine Fragen zu beantworten.

Sie übten Gitarre spielen.

Sie schlugen vor, einen Spaziergang zu machen.

Lösungen

1. Playing tennis is her favourite hobby.
He risked losing his life.
She stopped smoking and drinking.
Carl avoided answering my questions.
They practiced playing the guitar.
They suggested going for a walk.

Besondere Verbformen

Seite 37

> **Unbedingt merken:**
> Nach folgenden Präpositionen steht immer das Verb im Gerundium:
>
> | | | | |
> |---|---|---|---|
> | after | nach; nachdem | in spite of | obwohl |
> | before | bevor; vor | instead of | (an)statt |
> | besides | außer; abgesehen davon, daß | on | bei, als |
> | by | durch; wenn | without | ohne |
>
> On receiving the letter, Mrs Jones called her husband.
>
> Viele Substantive, Adjektive und Verben sind fest mit einer Präposition verbunden. Auch nach diesen Verbindungen steht das Gerundium.
> He stayed at home for fear of flying.   ... aus Angst vorm Fliegen.
> I'm afraid of flying.   Ich habe Angst vorm Fliegen.
> I insist on flying.   Ich bestehe darauf zu fliegen.

Substantive mit Präposition + Gerundium:

chance of	Gelegenheit zu	mistake of	Fehler zu
choice between	Wahl zwischen	possibility of	Möglichkeit zu
danger of	Gefahr zu	reason for	Grund für zu
difficulty in	Schwierigkeit zu	risk of	Risiko zu
for fear of	aus Angst vor	trouble in	Problem(e) mit
hope of	Hoffnung auf	way of	Art und Weise

1 Find the right preposition and add the gerund of the verb in brackets.

The chance _____ (catch) a fish today is very slim.

He made the mistake _____ (attack) me.

The probability _____ (meet) her again is not very high.

There's no possibility _____ (get) to Frankfurt in time today.

He is in danger _____ (be) killed in that country.

He's got some difficulty _____ (eat) Arabian food.

Ken hasn't lost hope _____ (win) some money on the horses.

There's no way _____ (know) if he's lying or not.

The risk _____ (lose) money is high if you invest in silver.

We had trouble _____ (find) the way.

They had the choice _____ (stay) or _____ (leave)

Lösungen

1. of catching
   of attacking
   of meeting
   of getting
   of being
   in eating
   of winning
   of knowing
   of losing
   in finding
   of staying or leaving

Besondere Verbformen

Adjektive mit Präposition + Gerundium:

to be afraid of	Angst haben vor
to be bad/good at	schlecht/gut sein in
to be fond of	gern (tun), mögen
to be frightened of	Angst haben vor
to be interested in	interessiert sein/Interesse haben an
to be keen on	gern (tun), darauf aus sein
to be proud of	stolz sein auf
to be sorry about/for	leid tun, daß

1 Put in the right preposition and add the gerund of the verb in brackets.

We're interested _____ (find) Canadian pen-friends.

I'm fond _____ (travel) by train.

I'm bad _____ (surf).

She's not very good _____ (learn) languages.

Peter is afraid _____ (tell) the truth.

I'm proud _____ (be) a European citizen.

I'm sorry _____ (shout) at you yesterday.

My mother is keen _____ (keep) her house very clean.

I'm frightened _____ (walk) through a dark forest.

I'm tired _____ (be) treated like a child.

Verben mit Präposition + Gerundium:

to apologize for	sich entschuldigen für
to believe in	glauben an, etwas halten von
to dream of/about	träumen von
to feel like	Lust haben auf/zu
to look forward to	sich freuen auf
to insist on	bestehen auf
to succeed in	Erfolg haben bei/mit, (es) schaffen
to talk about/of	sprechen über, reden von
to think of	denken an, in Betracht ziehen

Lösungen

1. in finding
   of travelling
   at surfing
   at learning
   of telling
   of being
   about / for shouting
   on keeping
   of walking
   of being

Besondere Verbformen

1 Complete the sentences with a matching verb from the list and add the gerund of the verb in brackets.

to apologize for, to believe in, to decide against, to dream of, to give up, to insist on, to look forward to, to succeed in, to talk about, to think of

I _____ (travel) to Samoa one day.

You should _____ (be) late again.

Peter _____ (begin) to learn English.

My husband _____ (buy) an expensive new car.

Bill _____ (pass) the test last Monday.

I've _____ (learn) everything in this book.

I _____ (tell) the truth.

John _____ (meet) her at once.

My wife _____ (buy) a new dress next week.

He _____ (see) you on Saturday.

Tips & Hilfen:
Wenn du nicht weißt, ob du einen Infinitiv oder ein Gerundium verwenden sollst, nimm den Infinitiv. Geht eine Präposition voran, nimm stets das Gerundium.

Das Gerundium steht immer nach folgenden Wendungen:

It's good fun walking in the rain.	Es macht viel Spaß, im Regen zu laufen.
It's no good complaining.	Es ist zwecklos, sich zu beschweren.
It's no use carrying on.	Es ist zwecklos weiterzumachen.
It's not worth doing.	Es lohnt sich nicht, es zu tun.
How / What about leaving now?	Wie wär's, wenn wir jetzt gingen?

Zusammenfassung:
- Das Gerundium kann die Funktion des Subjekts oder des Objekts im Satz übernehmen.
- Nach den meisten Präpositionen steht das Verb im Gerundium.
- Das Gerundium steht nach bestimmten Verben und Wendungen.

Lösungen

1. I'm dreaming of travelling
   apologize for being
   is talking about beginning
   decided against buying
   succeeded in passing
   given up learning
   believe in telling
   insists on meeting
   is thinking of buying
   He's looking forward to seeing

Participle – Partizip

> **Unbedingt merken:**
> Es gibt zwei Arten von Partizipien: *present participle* (Infinitiv + *-ing* / Partizip Präsens) und *past participle* (3rd form / Partizip Perfekt). Das *present participle* hat aktive Bedeutung, das *past participle* passive:
>
> | **Aktiv** | **Passiv** |
> |---|---|
> | Present participle | Past participle |
> | the sound of breaking glass | the broken glass |
> | das Geräusch zerbrechenden Glases | das zerbrochene Glas |
>
> Erweiterte Partizipien können Relativsätze ersetzen und verkürzen. Anders als im Deutschen muß ein erweitertes Partizip hinter dem Substantiv stehen, auf das es sich bezieht:
>
> **Present participle:**
> The man who is talking to Jake is my husband.
> The man talking to Jake is my husband.
>
> **Past participle:**
> That woman owned the house that was sold for £100,000.
> That woman owned the house sold for £100,000.

1 Shorten the sentences by using the present participle for active and the past participle for passive sentences.

There's a pretty salesgirl who sells picture postcards.

_____

I live in a house which was built in 1879.

_____

Cologne is a town which was founded by the Romans.

_____

The window which was broken by your son has to be paid for.

_____

The woman who cuts my hair has moved to another hairstylist's.

_____

The boys who are playing street hockey are my friends.

_____

Falcone was a judge who was killed by the Mafia in Sicily.

_____

Have you got anything in your pocket that doesn't belong to you?

_____

Lösungen

1. a pretty salesgirl selling picture postcards.
   a house built in 1879.
   a town founded by the Romans.
   The window broken by your son
   The woman cutting my hair
   The boys playing street hockey
   a judge killed by the Mafia
   in your pocket not belonging to you?

Besondere Verbformen

Tips & Hilfen:
Partizipien können an die Stelle von Nebensätzen treten, wenn bestimmte Voraussetzungen vorliegen:
- bei indirekten Zeitangaben:
  When Paul heard the Prince record, he had to dance.
  Hearing the Prince record, Paul had to dance.
  Als Paul die Platte von Prince hörte, mußte er tanzen.
  After he had done his homework, John went to town.
  Having done his homework, John went to town.
  Nachdem er seine Hausaufgaben gemacht hatte, ging John in die Stadt.
- bei Nennung eines Grundes:
  Because he felt ill, John decided not to play football.
  Feeling ill, John decided not to play football.
  Weil er sich krank fühlte, entschied sich John, nicht Fußball zu spielen.

1 Translate the following sentences using the present participle.

Nachdem sie ihre Briefe geschrieben hatte, ging sie nach Hause.

Weil ich mich müde fühlte, sagte ich ihr, daß ich nicht kommen könnte.

Als ich die Straße entlang ging, sah ich dich.

Weil wir auf dem Lande lebten, konnten wir nicht ins Kino gehen.

Nachdem er ein Glas Bier getrunken hatte, ging er ins Bett.

Nachdem wir ein Hotel gefunden hatten, suchten wir ein Restaurant.

Als Peter in London war, schaute er sich die Tower Bridge an.

Weil ich kein Auto habe, kann ich nicht in die Stadt fahren.

Weil ich nicht hungrig war, konnte ich nichts essen.

Als er aus dem Fenster schaute, sah er eine Katze im Baum sitzen.

Weil er arbeitslos ist, hat er nicht viel Geld.

Lösungen

1. Having written her letters, she went home.
   Feeling tired, I told her (that) I couldn't come.
   Walking along the road, I saw you.
   Living in the country, we couldn't go to the cinema.
   Having drunk a glass of beer, he went to bed.
   Having found a hotel, we looked for a restaurant.
   Being in London, Peter had a look at Tower Bridge.
   Not having a car, I can't drive into town.
   Not being hungry, I couldn't eat anything.
   Looking out of the window, he saw a cat sitting in a tree.
   Being unemployed, he hasn't got much money.

Besondere Verbformen

> **Unbedingt merken:**
> Nach *to go* und *to come* steht das *present participle*. Nach Verben der Wahrnehmung (*to feel, to hear, to listen to, to notice, to see, to watch, to smell* usw.) und nach *to catch, to find, to keep, to leave* folgt häufig die Konstruktion Objekt + *present participle*. In der deutschen Übersetzung steht ein Infinitiv oder ein Nebensatz mit *wie* oder *daß*:
> She heard her mum shouting.   Sie hörte ihre Mutter rufen.
> She saw him running home.   Sie sah, wie / daß er nach Hause lief.

1 Combine the following two sentences.

The girl was standing in front of the shop window. I saw her.

I saw the girl standing in front of the shop window.

He was walking up the hill at nine o'clock. Peter saw him.

The fans were shouting and singing in the streets. I heard them.

He was sitting on the sofa. That's where I found him.

Somebody was going down the stairs. I heard some steps.

The boys were playing hockey in the street. Ricky watched them for a while.

The child next door was screaming for hours last night. I heard him.

The birds were singing. But she didn't hear anything.

The choir was singing. We were listening.

Katy stole some chocolate out of the cupboard. Her mother caught her.

The meat was burning. I smelt it.

Carl ran down the street. That's when I noticed him.

Lösungen

1. Peter saw him walking up the hill at nine o'clock.
I heard the fans shouting and singing in the streets.
I found him sitting on the sofa.
I heard somebody going down the stairs.
For a while Ricky watched the boys playing hockey in the street.
I heard the child next door screaming for hours last night.
She didn't hear the birds singing.
We were listening to the choir singing.
Her mother caught Katy stealing some chocolate out of the cupboard.
I smelt the meat burning.
I noticed Carl running down the street.

Besondere Verbformen   *Seite 43*

> **Tips & Hilfen:**
> Wenn du mit den Partizipien Probleme hast, benutze Relativsätze oder von Konjunktionen eingeleitete Nebensätze.

1 Rewrite the sentences using the given conjunctions or relative pronouns.

I was woken up by a bell ringing next door.   *because*
I was woken up because a bell was ringing next door.

Jenny broke her arm playing tennis.   *while*
Jenny _____

I noticed a man knocking on the doors of all the houses.   *who*
I _____

Be careful crossing the road.   *when*
Be _____

Feeling tired she went to bed early last night.   *because*
She _____

Having finished her work she left the office.   *after* + past perfect
She _____

Being from Liberia she needs a visa to stay in this country.   *because*
She _____

I heard Susan locking the door.   *when*
I _____

Bob sat there listening to some strange music.   *and*
Bob _____

The men working on the high tower were in real danger.   *who*
_____

> **Zusammenfassung:**
> Partizipien stehen
> • anstelle von Relativsätzen,
> • anstelle von adverbialen Nebensätzen der Zeit und des Grundes,
> • nach bestimmten Verben.

Lösungen

1. Jenny broke her arm while she was playing tennis.
   I noticed a man who was knocking on the doors of all the houses.
   Be careful when you're crossing the road.
   She went to bed early last night because she felt tired.
   She left the office after she had finished her work.
   She needs a visa to stay in the country because she's from Liberia.
   I heard Susan when she was locking the door.
   Bob sat there and was listening to some strange music.
   The men who were working on the high tower were in real danger.

Seite 44

Besondere Verbformen

OKiDOKi?!

- Gerund or infinitive? Put in the right forms in the right tense.

Dear Caroline,

I know that you'd like _____ (know) more about me, my character, and my life. In spite of _____ (talk) things over on the telephone I've decided _____ (write) a letter to you. For me it's much easier _____ (write) everything down in a letter without _____ (have) someone around.

I'm not really interested in _____ (hit) the keys of a computer. _____ (watch) the moon and the stars at night is one of my hobbies. It's much better than _____ (stay) at home and _____ (watch) horror films on TV. I can understand people who dream of _____ (dance) in a disco. But that doesn't interest me. I need fresh air. That's why I dislike _____ (smoke) and _____ (stand) around in a room full of people. I'm not fond of loud music and _____ (hop) around.

I also like _____ (eat) Chinese food with chopsticks. If you know how _____ (use) them, _____ (eat) with chopsticks is much more fun than _____ (hold) a knife and fork.

I wonder if you're also interested in Chinese food, good meals and _____ (watch) the stars at night. I would like _____ (meet) you one day. Until I do, please keep on _____ (write) to me. I'd love _____ (get) to know you better. I will try _____ (write) again soon.

Yours, Oliver

Lösungen

- to know, having talked, to write, to write, having, hitting, Watching, staying, watching, dancing, smoking, standing, (of) hopping, eating, to use, eating, holding, watching, to meet, writing, to get, to write

Kapitel 3

Wichtige Satztypen

Seite 45

Complex sentences, also Satzgefüge, die aus Haupt- und Nebensätzen bestehen, unterscheiden sich im Englischen und Deutschen im Prinzip nicht voneinander.

Ein Problem ist jedoch die Entscheidung für das richtige Relativpronomen, und die Frage, ob es weggelassen werden darf oder nicht.

Fehlerträchtig ist außerdem die indirekte Rede *(reported speech)* und der Gebrauch des Passivs *(passive).*

Relative clauses – Relativsätze

> **Unbedingt merken:**
> Relativsätze *(relative clauses)* bestimmen das Substantiv näher, auf das sie sich beziehen, und werden meistens mit einem Relativpronomen *(relative pronoun)* eingeleitet. Wenn Relativsätze nicht weggelassen werden können, ohne daß der Sinn der Aussage verlorengeht, dann sind es notwendige Relativsätze *(defining relative clauses).* Sie werden nicht durch Kommas abgetrennt.
> Mrs. Brown is the lady **who** usually looks after our daughter when we go out.

	Relativpronomen als Subjekt	Relativpronomen als Objekt	Relativpronomen im Genitiv
Personen	who / that: The singer who / that was on TV is well known.	who / that: The man who / that I met is very famous.	whose: The man whose son fell ill is very rich.
Tiere / Dinge	which / that: The book which / that is very old is green.	which / that: Are these the books which / that you gave me?	whose: The house whose owner is an actor is very modern.

1 *Which, who* or *whose?*

Kangaroos are animals _____ live in Australia.

Is that the woman _____ wants to buy your car?

On Sunday I met a man _____ sister knows you.

The road _____ we followed ended near a lake.

I don't like dogs _____ bite.

I don't like people _____ lose their temper easily.

That's the boy _____ purse was stolen.

An orphan is a child _____ parents are dead.

This school is for kids _____ first language is Latin.

This is the house _____ my friend built in 1989.

Lösungen

1. which / that, who / that, whose, which / that, which / that, who / that, whose, whose, whose, which / that

Wichtige Satztypen

Tips & Hilfen:
Auf *whose* folgt immer ein Substantiv. *Whose* drückt einen Besitz oder eine Zugehörigkeit aus und läßt sich im Deutschen mit *dessen, deren* wiedergeben, wenn es ein Relativpronomen ist. Als einleitendes Fragewort wird es mit *Wessen* übersetzt: *Whose bag is this?*
Verwechsle nicht *whose* mit *who's* (= *who is*).

1 Combine the two sentences with *who*, *which*, *that* or *whose*.

He's an architect. – He designs bridges.

He's an architect who
_____

A woman answered the phone. – She said Paul wasn't there.

A woman
_____

Yesterday I met a nice girl. – Her mother writes novels.

_____

What's the name of the blonde girl? – She just came in.

_____

My father works for a high tech company. – It produces computers.

_____

There was a strike at the car factory in 1995. – It lasted for three weeks.

_____

I went to see the doctor. – He lives on the High Street.

_____

A widow is a woman. – Her husband is dead.

_____

Where is the cheese? – It was in the fridge.

_____

I have some good friends. – They live in Hamburg.

_____

Lösungen

1. He is an architect **who / that** designs bridges.
A woman answered the phone **who / that** said Paul wasn't there.
Yesterday I met a nice girl **whose** mother writes novels.
What's the name of the blonde girl **who / that** just came in?
My father works for a high tech company **which / that** produces computers.
There was a strike at the car factory last year **which / that** lasted for three weeks.
I went to see the doctor, **who / that** lives on the High Street.
A widow is a woman **whose** husband is dead.
Where is the cheese **which / that** was in the fridge?
I have some good friends **who / that** live in Hamburg.

Wichtige Satztypen

Seite 47

> **Unbedingt merken:**
> Nicht notwendige Relativsätze *(non-defining relative clauses)* enthalten Zusatzinformationen, die für das Verständnis einer Aussage entbehrlich sind. Sie werden durch Kommas abgetrennt.
>
> Mrs. Peabody, *who has caught a cold*, usually looks after our daughter.
>
> In nicht notwendigen Relativsätzen darf das Relativpronomen *that* nicht verwendet werden. Das bedeutet: Vor *that* steht nie ein Komma, da immer ein notwendiger Relativsatz folgt.

1 Mark all non-defining relative clauses by inserting commas.

It was a boring meeting. The chairman who was sitting to my right made the first speech. The speech which lasted more than 50 minutes was much too long. I remember a man who was standing in the back. He was trying to talk to a woman in a red dress who was very interested in the speech. But this woman whose name is Marylin only gave him a short smile. I could understand this man in the back who wasn't following the speech.

The chairman's speech which I was no longer listening to didn't come to an end. In fact, this terrible speech which had been written on 25 small pieces of paper went on and on.

I called the waiter who was standing beside the door and asked him to bring me some coffee. I thought the coffee would keep me awake. When the waiter came in with the tray he stumbled.

The waiter who had lost his balance couldn't hold the tray. The tray which he was balancing on one hand fell down. The coffee was all over the floor and the cup whose handle was broken couldn't be used anymore.

I was hoping that he would bring me another cup of fresh coffee. But he never appeared again.

> **Tips & Hilfen:**
> Wenn sich Relativpronomen auf Namen oder Vornamen beziehen, dann handelt es sich fast immer um nicht notwendige Relativsätze. Es wird also kein Komma gesetzt.

Lösungen

1. The chairman, who was sitting to my right, …
The speech, which lasted more than 50 minutes, …
… in a red dress, who was very interested …
But this woman, whose name is Marylin, …
The chairman's speech, which I was no longer listening to, …
… this terrible speech, which had been written on 25 small pieces of paper, …
… the waiter, who was standing beside the door, …
The waiter, who had lost his balance, …
The tray, which he was balancing on one hand, …
The cup, whose handle was broken, …

Wichtige Satztypen

Seite 48

Mr Miller's son who is twelve years old is fond of football.

Mr Miller's son, who is twelve years old, is fond of football.

1 Defining clause without a comma or non-defining clause with a comma?

Pupils who are lazy should leave this school.

Pupils who are late should apologize.

I've just met Mrs Ferguson who wants to buy a new dress.

The people who wanted to use the lift had assembled in front of the door.

The speech which lasted three hours was very boring.

My only brother who lives in Bremen is 42 years old.

It was the most exciting tennis match that I've ever seen.

The boy who you are looking at is my friend Bryan.

The German city of Munich which is in Bavaria is a very nice town.

This morning I met Fiona who I hadn't seen for ages.

The woman who lives next door is a hair stylist.

Do you have anything that belongs to me?

Lösungen

1. kein Komma
   kein Komma
   Komma
   kein Komma
   Kommas
   Kommas
   kein Komma
   kein Komma
   Kommas
   Komma
   kein Komma
   kein Komma

Unbedingt merken:
Die Relativpronomen *who, which* und *that* können entweder Subjekt oder Objekt in einem Relativsatz sein.

This is the book which I read on holiday. – Objekt
She's the lady who won a prize. – Subjekt

Tips & Hilfen:
Subjekt oder Objekt? Das Subjekt gibt Antwort auf die Frage: *Wer?* oder *Was?*, das Objekt auf *Wen?* oder *Was?*
Ist das Relativpronomen Subjekt des Satzes, dann folgt ein Verb.

Wichtige Satztypen

Seite 49

1 Underline those relative pronouns which are used as an object.

The girl who I met at the party is very attractive.

You're the man that I've been looking for.

This is the man who won the price.

What's the name of the film which you saw yesterday?

Do you remember the girl who you met at the station?

You're the friend who understands my problems best.

Jack is the man who she will marry in August.

Is this the plane which I can take to Heathrow?

He gave me the CD that I had asked for.

> **Unbedingt merken:**
> Wenn das Relativpronomen Objekt eines Satzes ist, kann es weggelassen werden. Das geht nur bei notwendigen Relativsätzen. Solche Sätze heißen *contact clauses*:
> the girl who / that I met at the party   —   the girl I met at the party

> **Tips & Hilfen:**
> Nach *everything, all, nothing, something, anything,* nach *first, last, only* und nach Superlativen *(easiest, funniest)* steht *that* immer im Objektfall. Es kann also immer wegfallen:
> the best book that I've ever read   —   the best book I've ever read

2 Underline those relative pronouns which are the object of the sentence and could be deleted.

This is the box which you wanted to have.

People who play golf have usually got plenty of money.

That's the man who you have to give the money to.

They gave their children everything that they wanted.

I wonder if he's the one who comes first.

I didn't meet anybody who I knew personally.

What's the name of the man who you met yesterday?

I don't like roses which are nearly black.

Have you found the keys that you lost?

She prefers flowers which have a nice smell.

Lösungen

1. who – Objekt
that – Objekt
who – Subjekt
which – Objekt
who – Objekt
who – Subjekt
who – Objekt
which – Objekt
that – Objekt

2. the box <u>which</u>
the man <u>who</u>
everything <u>that</u>
anybody <u>who</u>
the man <u>who</u>
the keys <u>that</u>

If-clauses – Bedingungssätze

> **Unbedingt merken:**
> Bedingungssätze (*if-clauses* oder *conditional clauses*) setzen sich aus einem *if*-Satz (dem Nebensatz) und einem Hauptsatz zusammen. Der *if*-Satz enthält – je nach Einschätzung des Sprechers – eine erfüllbare, eine wahrscheinlich nicht oder gar nicht erfüllbare Bedingung.

Would you lend me some money?	I need some money to buy cigarettes.	Why didn't you lend him any money?
I'll give you some money if you need it.	I'd lend you some money if you really needed it.	If he had needed it, I would have given him some money.
Typ 1: Der Hauptsatz beschreibt, was passiert / passieren kann.	**Typ 2:** Der Hauptsatz beschreibt, was passieren würde, wenn …	**Typ 3:** Der Hauptsatz beschreibt, was passiert wäre, wenn …

	Zeitform im if-Satz	Zeitform im Hauptsatz
Typ 1 erfüllbare Bedingung	present tense	*will*-future, ein Hilfsverb oder ein Imperativ
Typ 2 wahrscheinlich nicht erfüllbare Bedingung	simple past	*would / could / might* + Infinitiv
Typ 3 nicht erfüllbare Bedingung	past perfect	*would / could / might have* + past participle

Wichtige Satztypen *Seite 51*

1 Fill in *will* or *can* and the right form of the verb in the *if*-clause.

If it _____ (get) colder, I _____ (put on) a sweater.

If she _____ (work) hard, she _____ (pass) the examination.

We _____ (take) a taxi if I _____ (have) enough money.

If you _____ (not / hurry up), you _____ (miss) the train?

You _____ (earn) a lot of money if you _____ (do) what I say.

If Robert _____ (get) new information, he _____ (call) you at once.

If Patty _____ (not miss) the flight, she _____ (arrive) in time.

Tips & Hilfen:
Verwechsle nicht *if* mit *when*. *If* drückt eine logische Beziehung aus (falls A, dann B), *when* eine zeitliche Folge. *If* leitet Bedingungssätze ein, *when* leitet Nebensätze der Zeit ein:
When we reached our car, it had just stopped raining.
Das Wort *if* sollte mit *falls*, das Wort *when* mit *als* übersetzt werden.

2 Add *if* or *when*.

Tim knows that Scott is going to the USA and asks him _____ he plans to visit the United States. Scott answers: " _____ I have enough money by then, I'll be in Chicago in six weeks time." Tim wants to know _____ he has ever been there before. Scott replies that he was in New York _____ he was six years old. " _____ I first saw the huge skyscrapers I was really impressed." Tim: "I'll fly there too _____ there is any opportunity."

Tips & Hilfen:
Der *if*-Satz kann vor oder hinter dem Hauptsatz stehen. Aber merke dir: Geht der *if*-Satz voran, muß ein Komma dran.
Wichtig: Im *if*-Satz steht niemals *will* oder *would*!

Lösungen

1. gets – will put on
   works – will pass
   can / will take – have
   don't hurry up – will miss
   will earn – do
   gets – will call
   doesn't miss – will arrive

2. when, If, if, when, When, if

Wichtige Satztypen

> **Tips & Hilfen:**
> In *if*-Sätzen, die eine Bedingung enthalten, die nicht erfüllbar ist oder höchstwahrscheinlich nicht erfüllt wird, steht das *past tense,* nicht *would*:
> If I had time, I'd visit you.   Wenn ich Zeit hätte, würde ich dich besuchen.
>
> Statt *past tense* von *to be* (= *was*) steht mit *I, he, she, it* auch *were*:
> If I were a carpenter, ...

> **Unbedingt merken:**
> Bezieht sich der *if*-Satz auf eine allgemeingültige Tatsache, dann steht das *simple present* im *if*-Satz und im Hauptsatz:
> If it rains, you get wet.

1 Fill in the right forms: *will* + Verb or *would* + Verb.
Beachte, daß im *if*-Satz kein *will* oder *would* steht.

What _____ (you / do) if a pink elephant _____ (come) up to you?

If you (not / know) _____ how to ride, it _____ (not / be) much use having a horse.

I _____ (go) swimming even if you _____ (tell) me not to go.

If you _____ (listen) to me, you _____ (not / make) so many mistakes. But you never listen!

If you _____ (treat) him nicely, he _____ (do) anything for you.

If you _____ (eat) too much, you _____ (become) too fat.

If I _____ (be) President of the USA, I _____ (destroy) all military missiles.

Not me! I _____ (not / do) that if I _____ (be) you.

If there _____ (be) a party somewhere, we _____ (go) there.

Peter is not at home. He _____ (answer) the phone if he _____ (be) at home.

Lösungen

1. would you do – came
   don't know – is not
   will go – tell (auch möglich: would go – told)
   listened – would not
   treat – will do
   eat – will become
   were / was – would destroy
   wouldn't do – were / was
   was – would go (auch möglich: is – will go)
   would answer – was

Wichtige Satztypen **Seite 53**

1 Complete the sentences with the right form of the verbs in brackets.

Mother: What are your plans for Saturday?

Sheila: If the weather _____ (be) nice, I _____ (go) sailing.

Mother: And if the weather _____ (be) bad?

Sheila: Well, if the weather _____ (be) bad, I _____ (visit) a friend.

Mother: Oh! If that _____ (be) still Charlie, _____ (give) him my regards. By the way, I need some help.

Sheila: Sorry, Mum. If I _____ (have) time, I _____ (help) you but I have to leave now. Can you give me some money?

Mother: Sorry, dear. If I _____ (have) any money, I _____ (give) you some . But I haven't got any.

Sheila: Why don't you ask Dad? If he _____ (have) money, I'm sure he _____ (give) you enough for you and me.

Mother: Well, I'm sorry. If he _____ (have) money, he _____ (give) me some. But right now he hasn't got any.

Sheila: Life without money is terrible. I need some urgently. If I _____ (have) a gun, I _____ (rob) a bank.

Mother: But you haven't got a gun, dear. Why don't you stay at home?

Sheila: Come on, Mum. I have to go somewhere. If I _____ (stay) at home, I _____ (start) screaming. It's so boring at home.

Mother: You're a horrible girl. If I _____ (be) Dad, I _____ (not / give) you a penny. Why don't you leave school and start working? If you _____ (earn) money, you can _____ (spend) money, can't you?

Sheila: You're terrible. Sometimes I _____ (wonder) if you _____ (think) that I'm really wasteful. Didn't you have fun when you were young?

Lösungen

1. is – will go
   is
   is – will visit
   is – give
   had – would help
   had – would give
   has – will give
   had – would give
   had – would rob
   stay – will start / stayed – would start
   was / were – would not give
   earn – spend
   wonder – think

Reported Speech – Indirekte Rede

> **Unbedingt merken:**
> Die indirekte Rede gibt, begleitet von einem Einleitungssatz, wieder, was jemand gesagt hat:
>
> Tim: „I'm going home at six." Tim said he was going home at six.
>
> Wenn der Einleitungssatz im *simple past* steht, dann verschiebt sich die Zeitform von der direkten zur indirekten Rede um eine „Stufe" zurück *(back-shift)*:
>
> | | | |
> |---|---|---|
> | I do | → | I did |
> | I am doing | → | I was doing |
> | I have done | → | I had done |
> | I have been doing | → | I had been doing |
> | I did | → | I had done |
> | I had done | → | I had done (keine Verschiebung mehr möglich!) |
> | I'm going to do | → | I was going to do |
> | I will do | → | I would do |
> | I can do | → | I could do |
> | I may do | → | I might do |
>
> Steht im Einleitungssatz *present*, *present perfect* oder *future*, dann bleiben die Zeitformen der direkten Rede bei der Umformung in die indirekte Rede erhalten.

Oh, it's you, Yvonne.

Hi, Mum. I'm at the bus-stop.

I missed the bus.

I forgot about the time.

There'll be no more busses tonight.

Can Dad come and pick me up?

I won't be late again.

1 Yvonne's father asked his wife: "Was that Yvonne?"
Write mother's reply. Use reported speech. Use *add, admit, promise, say, tell*.

Lösungen

1. Yes, it was her. She told me that she was at the bus-stop. She said (that) she had missed the bus. She admitted (that) she had forgotten about the time.
She added (that) there were no more busses tonight.
She asked if you could go and pick her up.
She promised not to be late again.

Wichtige Satztypen

> **Unbedingt merken:**
> Wenn eine Aussage in der indirekten Rede allgemeingültig ist oder zum Zeitpunkt ihrer Wiedergabe noch zutreffend ist, dann bleibt die Zeitform der direkten Rede erhalten:
> Scott said: "It never rains in Southern California."
> Scott said it never rains in Southern California.

> **Tips & Hilfen:**
> Achte bei der Umformung in die indirekte Rede darauf, daß alle Pronomen und die Orts- und Zeitangaben an die Perspektive des neuen Sprechers angepaßt werden müssen.
> Das *that* nach dem Einleitungssatz kann stehen, wird besonders nach *say / tell* aber häufig weggelassen.
> Peter: "I have never seen you in our street before."
> Peter told me (that) he had never seen me in their street before.
> Henry: "Yesterday I met your sister here."
> Henry added (that) he had met my sister there the day before.

1 Rewrite the sentences in reported speech.

Ellen: "I'm so lonely."

Ellen told me _____

Bruce: "Sheila has gone to the hairdresser's."

Bruce said _____

Cliff: "I'll go to Martha's party on Saturday."

Cliff promised _____

Lester: "I can't help Roger with the repair work in your kitchen."

Lester was sorry _____

Patrick: "I've never seen such a computer maniac like you, Rick."

Patrick said _____

Sandra: "You're right, Mum."

Sandra admitted _____

Janine: "You never listen to what I say."

Janine complained _____

Sheila: "This church was built in the 11th century."

Sheila explained _____

Lösungen

1. ... (that) she was so lonely.
   ... (that) Sheila had gone to the hairdresser's.
   ... (that) he would go to Martha's party ...
   ... (that) he couldn't help Roger with the repair work in his kitchen.
   ... (that) he had never seen such a computer maniac like Rick.
   ... (that) her Mum was right.
   ... (that) I never listened to what she said.
   ... (that) this church had been built in the 11th century.

Seite 56 — Wichtige Satztypen

> **Unbedingt merken:**
> Fragewörter bleiben in der indirekten Rede erhalten. Es gibt keine Umschreibung mit *to do*. Fragen ohne Fragewort werden in der indirekten Rede mit *if* oder *whether* eingeleitet.
> Sarah asked Jeremy: „Where did you go?"
> Sarah asked Jeremy where he had gone.
> Sarah asked Jeremy: „Did you do the shopping?"
> Sarah asked Jeremy if / whether he had done the shopping.

1 Put the sentences into reported speech.

Lucy: „Have you got some candy for me, Brian?"

Lucy wanted to know if

My father: „Why are your test results so bad?"

My father wanted to know

„Were you successful?" I asked my friend.

I asked my friend

The bus-driver: „Where do you want to go?"

The bus-driver asked me

Dinah: „Why are you drinking so fast?"

She was wondering

„Why aren't you at school?" my mother wanted to know.

My mother

Peter: „Is it going to rain?"

Peter wanted to find out

Rose: „Where have all the people come from?"

Rose couldn't understand

Mum: „Have you already washed the car?"

My Mum asked my Dad

Elderly lady to a young man: „Can you help me, please?"

The elderly lady

Lösungen

1. … if Brian had some candy for her.
   … why my test results were so bad.
   … if he had been successful.
   … where I wanted to go.
   … why he was drinking so fast.
   … why I wasn't at school.
   … if it was going to rain.
   … where all the people had come from.
   … if he had already washed the car.
   … asked a young man if he could help her.

Wichtige Satztypen

Passive clauses – Passivsätze

> **Unbedingt merken:**
> Das Passiv wird mit einer Form von *to be* + *past participle* des Verbs gebildet. Bei der Verneinung steht *not* vor dem Verb.
> Ein und dieselbe Handlung läßt sich sprachlich als aktiver wie auch passiver Vorgang wiedergeben:
>
> | Henry | opened | the window. | *Aktiv* |
> | The window | was opened | (by Henry). | *Passiv* |
>
> Das Passiv wird verwendet, wenn es dem Sprecher nicht wichtig oder bekannt ist, wer der Handelnde ist. Der Handelnde wird nur dann (nach angehängtem *by*) genannt, wenn er für den Zusammenhang wichtig ist:
> This play was written <u>by Shakespeare</u>.

1 Frank had a passive role in this situation. Therefore use the passive.

First Tom only teased Frank. → First Frank was only teased (by Tom).

Then he called him a liar. → _____

Afterwards he hit him twice. → _____

He hit him on the nose. → _____

Then he kicked Frank. → _____

He kicked him very hard. → _____

He didn't kill Frank. → _____

But he really injured him. → _____

Nobody helped Frank. → _____

Someone called an ambulance. → _____

It took Frank to hospital. → _____

There the doctors looked after him. → _____

His classmates visited him. → _____

Later his parents took him home. → _____

> **Unbedingt merken:**
> Bei Verben, die fest mit einer Präposition verbunden sind – z.B. *to look after, to leave behind, to leave on, to talk about, to think of, to throw away* – wird die Präposition im Passivsatz nicht vom Verb getrennt, sondern steht direkt dahinter.

Lösungen

1. Then he was called a liar.
   Afterwards he was hit twice.
   He was hit on the nose.
   Then Frank was kicked.
   He was kicked very hard.
   Frank wasn't killed.
   But he was really injured.
   Frank wasn't helped by anybody.
   An ambulance was called.
   Frank was taken to hospital.
   There he was looked after by the doctors.
   He was visited by his classmates.
   Later he was taken home by his parents.

Seite 58   **Wichtige Satztypen**

1 Use the active or the passive. Mind the tenses!

Most of the Indian tribes _____ (vanish) from the prairies. The prairies _____ (use) as farmland, to build roads and towns. Only small parts of the prairies _____ (survive).

Now some Midwest states are trying to save what _____ (leave), or recreate what _____ (die out) in the wild.

In Dakota, for example, the former Sioux territory, most of today's wheat _____ (grow). The large farms _____ (run) by farmers who _____ (use) big machines. Farming _____ (industrialize) since the last century. Of course, the breeding of cattle _____ (mechanize), too. As a result, cowboys _____ (not / need) any more.

Horses _____ (ride) in rodeos. That's where the modern cowboy _____ (earn) his money. If he _____ (not / throw) off the horse, his ride _____ (be) a good show.

> **Tips & Hilfen:**
> Im Englischen wird das Passiv weit häufiger als im Deutschen verwendet. Für deutsche Aktivsätze, die mit *man* umschrieben sind, wird im Englischen das Passiv verwendet:
> *I was informed.* – *Man hat mich informiert.*

> **Unbedingt merken:**
> Welche Zeitform in Passivsätzen stehen muß, hängt vom Zusammenhang ab. Die Regeln dafür unterscheiden sich nicht vom Aktiv:
>
> | | | |
> |---|---|---|
> | *Many cars are stolen every day.* | immer → | simple present |
> | *One car has been stolen today.* | bisher → | present perfect |
> | *Tomorrow more cars will be stolen.* | künftig → | will + be + past part. |
>
> Handlungen, die gerade vor sich gehen, müssen – wie im Aktiv – in der *progressive form* stehen. Sie wird im Passiv mit *being* gebildet:
>
> | | | |
> |---|---|---|
> | *The car is being washed.* | zur Zeit → | present progressive |
> | *The car was being washed.* | gestern → | past progressive |

Lösungen

1. have vanished
   are used / have been used / are being used
   have survived
   has been left
   has died out
   is grown
   are run
   use
   has been industrialized
   has been mechanized
   aren't needed
   are ridden
   earns
   isn't thrown off
   is

Wichtige Satztypen **Seite 59**

1 Form passive sentences with the given tenses.

Banks / always / rob. *(future)* → Banks will always be robbed.

Excuse the mess. The house / paint. *present progressive*

The bridge / finish / by next May. *will-future*

The poor girl / not / look after / by her mother. *present perfect*

The rabbit likes / look at / by little children. *present progressive*

I felt as if I / watch / by the secret service. *past progressive*

The lawyer told me that Paul / put / in prison. *past perfect*

Please go away. I want to / alone / leave. *simple present*

Her record / next year / release. *will-future*

His best thriller / last year / publish. *simple past*

The letter / send / to the wrong address. *present perfect*

Unbedingt merken:

Neben Verben mit einem Objekt gibt es auch solche mit zwei Objekten, einem direkten und einem indirekten. Bei der Umformung vom Aktiv ins Passiv wird – anders als im Deutschen – das indirekte Objekt des Aktivsatzes zum Subjekt des Passivsatzes:

subject	predicate	indirect object	direct object
Her father	promised	Elenor	a trip to Spain.
Jhr Vater	versprach	Elenor	eine Spanienreise.
Elenor	was promised		a trip to Spain.
Eine Spanienreise	wurde	Elenor	versprochen.

Zu den Verben, die zwei Objekte haben können, gehören zum Beispiel:
to ask, to allow, to bring, to give, to offer, to order, to pay, to promise, to show, to teach, to tell, to write.

Lösungen

1. Excuse the mess. The house is being painted.
   The bridge will be finished by next May.
   The poor girl hasn't been looked after by her mother.
   The rabbit likes being looked at by little children.
   I felt as if I was being watched by the secret service.
   The lawyer told me that Paul had been put in prison.
   Please go away. I want to be left alone.
   Her record will be released next year.
   His best thriller was published last year.
   The letter has been sent to the wrong address.

Wichtige Satztypen

> **Tips & Hilfen:**
> Wenn das indirekte Personenobjekt ein Personalpronomen ist (*me, him, her* usw.) wird es im Passiv als Subjekt natürlich in den Nominativ gesetzt: *I, he, she* usw.:
> He told her a story.   She was told a story.

1 Form passive sentences.

She taught him English. → He was taught English.

They'll give her plenty of time to write the computer program.
She _____

Has somebody already shown you the photos?
Have you _____

They paid them £250 for the job.
_____

The American people elected him President of the USA.
_____

The ambassador invited us to the party.
_____

The boss has offered her a better job.
_____

The coach allowed me to play for twenty minutes.
_____

They called him the most dangerous terrorist in the Middle East.
_____

My brother promised me a copy of his book.
_____

The new company payed him £60,000 a year.
_____

The waiter served us a wonderful steak.
_____

Our teacher allowed us to go home.
_____

Lösungen

1. She will be given plenty of time to write the computer program.
   Have you already been shown the photos?
   They were paid £250 for the job.
   He was elected President of the USA (by the American people).
   We were invited to the party by the ambassador.
   She has been offered a better job (by her boss).
   I was allowed to play for twenty minutes.
   He was called the most dangerous terrorist in the Middle East.
   I was promised a copy of his book (by my brother).
   He was paid £60,000 a year by the new company.
   We were served a wonderful steak (by the waiter).
   We were allowed to go home.

Kapitel 4

Wortarten

Im Englischen gibt es genau dieselben Wortarten wie im Deutschen. Mit den meisten verhält es sich auch ganz genau so wie im Deutschen: Verben werden konjugiert, Substantive (Nomen), Pronomen, Adjektive und Artikel werden dekliniert, Präpositionen geben Verhältnisse an, Konjunktionen verbinden Satzteile oder Sätze usw.

Fehlerträchtig und deshalb zum Üben empfohlen sind die Wortarten, bei denen nicht alles ganz genau so ist, wie du es aus dem Deutschen gewohnt bist. Besonders gilt das

- für die Pluralbildung und die Verwendung des Artikels bei Substantiven,
- für die Stellung der Adverbien im Satz,
- für die Verwendung der jeweils richtigen Präposition,
- für die Verwendung der jeweils richtigen Konjunktion.

Nouns – Nomen / Substantive

Unbedingt merken:
Es gibt zählbare Substantive *(countables)* und nicht zählbare Substantive *(uncountables).* Die zählbaren haben Pluralformen und können mit dem unbestimmten Artikel *a* und mit Zahlwörtern *(one / two / …)* stehen. Der Plural der meisten zählbaren Substantive wird durch Anhängen von *-s* gebildet. Es gibt aber Ausnahmen:

-o	→ -oes	hero – heroes	aber:	**photos, kilos, radios**
-y	→ -ies	city – cities		
-ch	→ -ches	match – matches		
-f(e)	→ -ves	calf – calves	aber:	**roofs, beliefs**

1 Form the plural.

ox _____   goose _____   fish _____

child _____   tooth _____   foot _____

woman _____   mouse _____   echo _____

tomato _____   penny _____   thief _____

sheep _____   deer _____   man _____

berry _____   louse _____   knife _____

shelf _____   wolf _____   party _____

Lösungen

1. oxen, geese, fish / fishes, children, teeth, feet, women, mice, echoes, tomatoes, pennies / pence, thieves, sheep, deer, men, berries, lice, knives, shelves, wolves, parties

Wortarten

Unbedingt merken:

Maß- und Mengenangaben werden als Einheit betrachtet und stehen deshalb immer im Singular:

It's five miles into town.   *Is £50 enough?*

Nicht zählbare Substantive haben keinen grammatischen Plural. Sie werden als Singular behandelt, mit ihnen verbundene Verben stehen im Singular. Durch Zusätze wie *a piece / bottle / packet / cup of* werden solche Substantive zählbar und können mit Verben im Singular oder Plural stehen:

A piece of furniture is not enough.   *Two loaves of bread are enough.*

1 Form a sentence with each of the following uncountables.

advice	*Ratschlag*	knowledge	*Kenntnis(se)*
bread	*Brot*	news	*Nachricht(en), Neuigkeit(en)*
food	*Lebensmittel*	progress	*Fortschritt(e)*
information	*Information*	tea	*Tee*
homework	*Hausaufgaben*	water	*Wasser*
furniture	*Möbel*	holiday	*Ferien*
milk	*Milch*	cattle	*Vieh*

Die folgenden Substantive stehen immer im Plural; das gilt auch für mit ihnen verbundene Verben:

arms	*Waffen*	goods	*Ware(n)*
barracks	*Kaserne*	riches	*Reichtum*
cattle	*Vieh*	stairs	*Treppe*
clothes	*Kleidung*	surroundings	*Umgebung*
contents	*Inhalt*	wages	*Lohn*
people	*Leute*	police	*Polizei*
trousers	*Hose*	glasses	*Brille*
headphones	*Kopfhörer*	jeans	*Jeans*
shorts	*Shorts*	scissors	*Schere*
socks	*Socken*	tights	*Strumpfhose*

2 Singular or plural? Underline the right answer.

The cattle is / are in the field.

Many people lost their life / lives.

Sports is / are a popular subject.

Where is / are my jeans?

None of the girls like / likes Maths.

The news was / were bad.

The barracks is / are new.

Great damage was / were done.

The stairs are / is high.

The police has / have arrived.

My wages is / are very high.

Arms are / is delivered.

These people are / is rich.

The people of the Inca is / are extinct.

Lösungen

1. For example:
   Good advice isn't cheap.
   My knowledge of English isn't good.
   Bread is becoming expensive.
   The news sounds good.
   This food wasn't healthy.
   Good progress has been made.
   The information is useful.
   Would you like a cup of tea?
   There's a lot of homework to do.
   Two glasses of water, please.
   Our furniture is new.
   I spent my holiday in Spain last year.
   I'll drink a cup of milk.
   Cowboys are riding with the cattle.

2. The cattle are in the field.
   Many people lost their lives.
   Sports is a popular subject.
   Where are my jeans?
   None of the girls likes Maths.
   The news was bad.
   The barracks are new.
   Great damage was done.
   The stairs are high.
   The police have arrived.
   My wages are very high.
   Arms are delivered.
   These people are rich.
   The people of the Inca is extinct.

Wortarten

Seite 63

1 Translate the following sentences. Is the singular or plural needed?

Die Nachrichten waren schlecht.

Die meisten Ratschläge werden ignoriert.

Ihre Englischkenntnisse sind gut.

Sind 20 Pfund nicht zu schwer?

Ich muß zwei Brote kaufen.

Er hat keine Erfahrungen mit Computern.

Kunst ist ein beliebtes Schulfach.

Politik ist kompliziert.

> **Unbedingt merken:**
> Englische Substantive haben in der Regel kein besonderes grammatisches Geschlecht *(gender)*. Das biologische Geschlecht bestimmt das grammatische und läßt sich oft nur am Namen, am Personal- oder Possessivpronomen ablesen oder wird durch Zusätze wie *male / female* deutlich gemacht:
> Sue goes to see her best friend. She wants to see him and his new car.
> We have more female than male teachers at our school.
> Tiere werden als Dinge betrachtet, sie haben sächliches Geschlecht; es sei denn, sie sind persönliche Freunde (Haustiere). Schiffe und Länder werden als weiblich betrachtet.

2 Fill in the right pronoun.

She saw a black cat. _____ crossed her path from left to right.

My cat's name is Pussy. _____ is three years old.

There's the Cutty Sark. _____ was one of the best ships ever built.

In 1776, England lost _____ so-called first empire, the American colonies.

Lösungen

1. The news was bad.
   Most advice is ignored.
   Her knowledge of English is good.
   Isn't 20 pounds too heavy?
   I have to buy two loaves of bread.
   He has no experience with computers.
   Arts is a popular school subject.
   Politics is complicated.

2. ... a black cat. It crossed her path ...
   ... Pussy. She is ...
   ... the Cutty Sark. She was one of the best ships ...
   ... England lost her so-called first empire ...

Wortarten

Unbedingt merken:
Der *s-genitive* gibt an, wem etwas gehört. Er wird auch bei Tieren, Staaten, Städten und Institutionen verwendet. Das *s* wird an den Singular des Substantivs mit Apostroph angehängt. Ebenso ist es bei Substantiven, deren Plural ohne -s endet. Nach Plural -(e)s steht lediglich der Apostroph:
My friend's bicycle.   *The children's toys.*   *The boys' room.*
Auch Zeitangaben können ein Genitiv-s haben: *yesterday's papers.*
Der *of-genitive* gibt an, welcher Sache etwas zugeordnet ist. Er steht vor Dingen, Maß- und Mengenangaben sowie in bestimmten Wendungen:
The departure of the plane.   *One litre of milk.*   *A member of the team.*

1 Join the nouns. Sometimes the singular, sometimes the plural is used.

a bird / nest _____   the windows / house _____

Ann / mother _____   yesterday / newspaper _____

my parents / car _____   our neigbours / garden _____

the dog / name _____   the name / the street _____

a week / holiday _____   the company / success _____

the back / car _____   the children / toys _____

the top / the page _____   my father / birthday _____

the end / the book _____   ten minutes / a walk _____

a butcher / shop _____   the result / match _____

Unbedingt merken:
Der *definite article (the)* und der *indefinite article (a / an)* unterscheiden nicht nach Geschlecht oder Zahl. Der bestimmte Artikel wird nur gebraucht, wenn jemand oder etwas besonders hervorgehoben werden soll. Bei allgemein gebrauchten Substantiven steht kein Artikel:
We learnt about the life of Winston Churchill.   *Sometimes life is easy.*
The day I learnt how to swim.   *Saturday was a nice day.*
The children went home.   *Children like to play.*
Der bestimmte Artikel steht mit
- Namen von Inseln, Flüssen, Meeren, einigen Gebirgen und Ländern:
  the Isle of Wight, the Thames, the North Sea, the Alps, the Rocky Mountains, the United Kingdom,…
- Namen, die mit einem of-Genitiv zusammengesetzt sind:
  the House of Commons, the Tower of London,…
- Schiffsnamen:
  the Titanic, the Queen Elizabeth,…
- vielen Namen von Museen und Theatern:
  the British Museum, the Royal Albert Hall,…

Lösungen

1. a bird's nest
   the windows of the house
   Ann's mother
   yesterday's newspaper
   my parents' car
   our neighbours' garden
   the dog's name
   the name of the street
   a week's holiday
   the company's success /
   the success of the company
   the back of the car
   the children's toys
   the top of the page
   my father's birthday
   the end of the book
   a ten minutes' walk
   a butcher's shop
   the result of the match

Wortarten

1 With or without article? Cross out the wrong part of the sentence.

After the accident Peter was taken to hospital / to the hospital.

She doesn't belong to high society / the high society of Great Britain.

More and more people think that they have to hate society / the society.

Conquering space / the space has been a dream of mankind / the mankind.

You'll be lucky if you find work / the work at the steel works.

He's serving thirty years in prison / in the prison.

He has been working at prison / at the prison for nearly thirty years.

If you suffer from Saturday night fever you should go to town / to the town.

He goes to church / to the church every Sunday.

We'll travel to London by plane / by the plane.

Unbedingt merken:
Im Gegensatz zum Deutschen steht der unbestimmte Artikel vor:
- Bezeichnungen für Berufe: Neil Armstrong was an astronaut.
- Nationalitäten: James Joyce was an Irishman.
- Mitgliedschaft in Gruppen – außer bei Titeln oder Ämtern, die einzigartig sind:
  Rob is a member of our football team. aber:
  George Washington became President of the United States of America.
- vor Zeit-, Mengen- und Maßangaben in der Bedeutung von „pro":
  He goes swimming once a month.   I work five days a week.

---

2 Translate these expressions using *a / an* or *the* where necessary.

einmal im Monat

ein halbes Pfund Butter

sieben Tage in der Woche

die meisten Leute

die ganze Zeit

ein Viertel des Kuchens

die beiden grünen Kleider

gerade die richtige Menge

ein paar Studenten

zweimal am Tag

Architekt sein

Lösungen

1. to hospital (Zweck des Gebäudes, kein bestimmtes Krankenhaus)
the high society (eine bestimmte Gesellschaft(sschicht))
society (allgemein)
space (allgemein)
mankind (die Menschheit allgemein)
work (allgemein)
in prison (Zweck des Gebäudes, kein bestimmtes Gefängnis)
at the prison (in diesem bestimmten Gefängnis)
to town (keine bestimmte Stadt)
to church (Zweck des Gebäudes, keine bestimmte Kirche)
by plane (allgemein)

2. once a month
half a pound of butter
seven days a week
most (of the) people
all the time / the whole time
a quarter of the cake
both the green dresses
just the right amount
a few (of the) students
twice a day
to be an architect

Adverbs – Adverbien

> **Unbedingt merken:**
> Adjektive *(adjectives)* beschreiben Lebewesen, Dinge oder Ereignisse. Sie bestimmen Substantive oder Pronomen näher und stehen entweder vor dem Substantiv oder nach Verben, die einen Zustand oder eine Eigenschaft ausdrücken:
> *to be, to feel, to look, to smell, to sound, to taste,…*
> Mary is pretty.   She is pretty.   She is a pretty girl.   She looks pretty.

> **Tips & Hilfen:**
> Aus Adjektiven abgeleitete Adverbien werden durch Anhängen von *-ly* gebildet. Dabei sind folgende Besonderheiten zu beachten:
>
> | | | |
> |---|---|---|
> | die Endung *-y* wird zu *-ily* | easy – | easily |
> | die Endung *-le* wird zu *-ly* | simple – | simply |
> | die Endung *-ic* wird zu *-ically* | fantastic – | fantastically |
> | die Endung *-ly* wird zu *in a way /manner* | friendly – | in a friendly way |
>
> Neben diesen abgeleiteten gibt es ursprüngliche Adverbien, die die gleiche Form wie Adjektive haben, z. B.:
> *close, far, daily, weekly, early, long, little, fast, low, straight,…*
>
> Manche Adverbien haben zwei Formen mit unterschiedlicher Bedeutung:
> **bad** *(schlecht)* – **badly** *(sehr, dringend)*   **hard** *(schwer)* – **hardly** *(kaum)*
> **dead** *(tot, völlig)* – **deadly** *(tödlich)*   **high** *(hoch)* – **highly** *(höchst)*
> **terrible** *(schrecklich)* – **terribly** *(äußerst)*   **late** *(spät)* – **lately** *(kürzlich)*
> **free** *(frei, gratis)* – **freely** *(frei, ungehindert)*   **fair** *(fair)* – **fairly** *(ziemlich)*
>
> Das Adverb zu *good* ist *well*.

1 Adverb or adjective? Use the words from the list – if possible only once.

bad(ly), careful(ly), crazy (crazily), dangerous(ly), fast, happy (happily), nervous(ly), quiet(ly), usual(ly), good – well, wonderful(ly)

My parents are both _____ and a bit _____. You know, they've been _____ married for nearly twenty years. They know each other very _____. They need each other _____. Well, my father is a very _____ driver. He drives _____ when my mother is sitting in the car, you know. It's not that you have to sit _____ in the car because he drives too _____. He is a very _____ driver. My mother doesn't like _____ driving. When my father is too _____, she _____ tells him to slow down a little bit. That's what he _____ does then.

Lösungen

1. wonderful
   crazy
   happily
   well
   badly
   fast
   carefully
   nervously
   dangerously
   good
   dangerous
   fast
   quietly
   usually

Z.T. sind die Wörter auch anders einsetzbar.

Wortarten

1 Translate the following sentences.

Er ist ein hochbezahlter Manager. Die Firma braucht ihn dringend.

Ich kenne ihn sehr gut. Seine Lieder sind ziemlich schlecht.

Sie ist eine hübsche Frau, aber sie ist auch ziemlich arrogant.

Ich bin ziemlich sicher, daß er ein Drogenhändler ist.

Klettere so hoch du kannst. Der Berg ist äußerst schwer zu besteigen.

Es ist höchst faszinierend, dich die Tür anmalen zu sehen.

Was du sagst, ist wirklich gut, aber ich kann nicht zuhören. Ich bin todmüde.

Unbedingt merken:
Adverbien beschreiben eine Handlung. Sie beziehen sich daher häufig auf Verben, aber auch auf Adjektive, andere Adverbien oder den ganzen Satz:
Scott plays soccer well.   His physical condition is extremely good.
Scott didn't play very well. Fortunately he is a member of our rival club.
Die Stellung der Adverbien am Satzanfang *(front position)*, in der Satzmitte *(mid position)* und am Satzende *(end position)* hängt von der Betonung und der Art der Adverbien ab.

Am Satzanfang (vor dem Subjekt):
- Adverbien, die sich auf den ganzen Satz beziehen. Dazu gehören:
  actually, obviously, evidently, hopefully, perhaps, possibly, surely,...
  Fortunately all students passed the final exam.
- Adverbien, die Sätze miteinander verknüpfen. Dazu gehören:
  first(ly), second(ly), then, finally, indeed, in contrast, after all, however, anyway,...
  It was cold. Anyway we had a good time.
- Adverbien der bestimmten Zeit, wenn sie betont werden sollen. Dazu gehören:
  yesterday, today, tomorrow,...
  Tomorrow we are going to the cinema.

Lösungen

1. He's a highly paid manager. The firm needs him badly.
I know him very well. His songs are pretty terrible (bad).
She's a pretty woman, but she's also pretty arrogant.
I'm pretty sure (that) he is a drug dealer.
Climb as high as you can. The mountain is extremely (terribly) difficult to climb.
It's highly fascinating to see you painting the door.
What you say is really good, but I can't listen. I'm dead tired.

Seite 68 — Wortarten

In der Satzmitte (zwischen Subjekt und Vollverb bzw. hinter dem Hilfsverb):
- Adverbien der unbestimmten Zeit und Häufigkeit. Dazu gehören:
  always, ever, just, never, often, seldom, soon, sometimes, usually, …
  Robert usually comes home late. I've never heard this before.

Am Satzende (hinter Verb und Objekt):
- Adverbien der Art und Weise. Dazu gehören die meisten abgeleiteten Adverbien wie
  carefully, naturally, properly, possibly, simply, seriously, well,…
  You have to read the book carefully.
- Adverbien des Ortes. Dazu gehören:
  here, everywhere, outside,…
  They spent their holidays here.
- Adverbien der bestimmten Zeit. Dazu gehören:
  yesterday, tonight, tomorrow,…
  They will come and visit us the day after tomorrow.
- Adverbien der bestimmten Häufigkeit. Dazu gehören:
  daily, weekly, once,…
  To understand the meaning, you have to read the article twice.

---

1   Form sentences. Put adverbs of place before adverbs of time.

The Perkins / for a long time / have lived / in that house.

The Perkins _____

My wife / every Friday / to the bank / goes

My wife _____

You'll meet / in Bristol / my partner / next week

You'll meet _____

He / this morning / in the garden / worked / hard

He _____

Our team / well / played / last week / in the match

Our team _____

I'll be / from ten / in the office / to five / tomorrow

I'll be _____

I / in the library / yesterday / an interesting book / found

I _____

Eileen / take / will / the / to / zoo / Sunday / next / friends / her

Eileen _____

Lösungen

1. The Perkins have lived in that house for a long time.
   (Every Friday) My wife goes to the bank every Friday.
   You'll meet my partner in Bristol next week.
   (This morning) He worked hard in the garden this morning.
   (Last week) Our team played well in the match last week.
   (Tomorrow) I'll be in the office from ten to five tomorrow.
   (Yesterday) I found an interesting book in the library yesterday.
   (Next Sunday) Eileen will take her friends to the zoo next Sunday.

Wortarten **Seite 69**

> **Unbedingt merken:**
> Wenn verschiedene Adverbien aufeinander folgen, so gilt:
> Erst Art und Weise, dann Ort, dann zuletzt Zeit.
> Niemals dürfen Verb und Objekt durch Adverbien getrennt werden.
> He plays ~~well~~ soccer well.

1 Form sentences.

on Sundays / play / we / often / squash /
but / on a Monday / have / we / never / played

slowly / Peter / the safe / opened /
he / so much money / never / before / had / seen

Susan / has / in her life / never / a good idea / had

when / I / a kid / was / climbed / I / often / trees

she / has / always / helpful / been /
she / helps / her father / in the shop / twice a week

one day / started / Sandra / jogging /
you / can see / every morning / in the park / her

have / you / ever / a pink crocodile / seen / ? /
I've / one / seen / never

I / forget / never / birthday / my sister's /
But / she / forgets / always / mine

the meetings / take / often / in a restaurant / place

Lösungen

1. (On Sundays) We often play squash on Sundays.
   But we have never played on a Monday.
   Peter slowly opened the safe. He had never seen so much money before.
   Susan has never had a good idea in her life.
   When I was a kid, I often climbed trees.
   She has always been helpful. She helps her father in the shop twice a week.
   One day Sandra started jogging.
   (Every morning) You can see her in the park every morning.
   Have you ever seen a pink crocodile?
   I've never seen one.
   I never forget my sister's birthday.
   But she always forgets mine.
   The meetings often take place in a restaurant.

Seite 70 — *Wortarten*

> 💡 **Unbedingt merken:**
> Adverbien des Grades können sich auf bestimmte Wörter beziehen und stehen dann direkt vor den Bezugswörtern. Dazu gehören: *almost, completely, extremely, rather, totally, very,…*
> The plot of the story was rather disappointing.
> Die Adverbien *a bit, a little, a lot, very much* stehen immer am Satzende:
> I like her a lot.

1 Fill in the blanks using the following adverbs.

actually, almost, already, always, even, moreover, nearly, on the one hand, on the other hand, once, perfectly, still

Mother: Oh, it's you, Ellen. What a surprise! As you know, it's _____ past one o'clock in the morning. I _____ tell you to be in by midnight. _____ you say that you're old enough to go to a disco, but _____ you don't know when a fourteen-year-old teenager has to leave.

But has our young lady _____ looked at her watch? She likes to stay out late. _____, she likes to visit discos.

Ellen: What do you mean? I'm _____ fifteen and one o'clock is not late at all. _____ everybody else stays there till five in the morning. The others are _____ in the disco.

Mother: You know _____ well what I mean, my dear. _____, you're bad at school. That's why you have to work over the weekend.

And you haven't looked at your books _____

Lösungen

1. already
   always
   On the one hand
   on the other hand
   even
   Moreover
   nearly
   Almost
   still
   perfectly
   Actually
   once

Wortarten

Prepositions – Präpositionen

> **Unbedingt merken:**
> *Prepositions* sind Verhältniswörter. Sie geben an, in welchem zeitlichen, räumlichen oder sonstigen Verhältnis eine Person oder Sache zu einer anderen Person oder Sache steht.
> Viele Verben und Adjektive fordern eine ganz bestimmte Präposition. Leider gibt es da zwischen dem Deutschen und dem Englischen manche Unterschiede:
> I go to Hannover by train.   Ich fahre mit dem Zug nach Hannover.
> I stay with my aunt.   Ich bleibe bei meiner Tante.
>
> Da hilft nur, die wichtigsten Kombinationen auswendig zu lernen.

---

in, into, to, at, on, from, from … to   (in, im, von, an, am, auf, zu, von … bis)

direction (Richtung)
Jane goes into the classroom.
Paula goes to her friend.
He came from the doctor's.

place (Ort)
Paul is in the classroom.
She is at the station.
The book is on the table.

time (Zeitpunkt)
I saw him leave at midnight.
He was born in 1980.
He'll come on Sunday.

time (Zeitraum)
We camped there from May to June.
He lived there in 1980.
Stars are visible on clear nights.

---

1 Fill in the right prepositions.

Did you know all the people who were _____ our party?

I'd like to go _____ the new restaurant round the corner.

He went _____ the garden to water the flowers.

We'll visit you _____ Monday.

I don't want to eat hamburgers _____ a fast food restaurant.

Why don't we go _____ the cinema tonight?

Her bag is _____ the table.

There's no use in staying _____ the hall. The concert is over.

Your sister is still _____ the doctor's.

You can play basketball _____ eight _____ ten, if you like.

Why don't you call me _____ six o'clock tomorrow?

There's a present _____ your uncle on the table.

Lösungen

1. at our party
   to the new restaurant
   into the garden
   on Monday
   at a … restaurant
   to the cinema
   on the table
   in the hall
   at the doctor's
   from eight to ten
   at six o'clock
   from your uncle

Seite 72 — *Wortarten*

---

by, with, at (von, mit, bei, …)

instrument (Mittel)
He goes to school **by** car.
He writes **with** a pen.

place (Aufenthalt)
He lives **with** his aunt.
She is **with** her uncle.

cause (Urheber, Verursacher)
The book is **by** Grisham.
He was injured **by** a stone.

target (Ziel)
She smiles **at** me.
He shot an arrow **at** the target.

---

1 Find the missing prepositions.

My friend Harry usually goes to work _____ taxi.

He killed the spider _____ a stone.

Can I help you _____ anything?

Where is Pete? He's _____ his aunt at the moment.

He's looking _____ you.

Perhaps you would like to spend the holiday _____ me.

The horror story was written _____ Stephen King.

I left the keys _____ my wallet.

---

like, as, such as (als, wie, wie z. B., …)

comparison (Vergleich)
I'm **like** my brother.
You're clever **like** a professor.

example (Beispiel)
Rich people **such as** my aunt…
Girls **like** you…

instrument (Mittel)
She used her shoe **as** a hammer.

job (Beruf)
My brother works **as** a butcher.

---

2 Fill in the correct preposition.

She's a teacher, _____ my brother.

A few years ago I worked _____ a bus driver.

Everybody is ill at the moment. Our house is _____ a hospital.

My sister works _____ a nurse.

I want to do something nice, _____ going to the party.

She sings _____ a professional.

Materials _____ paper should be recycled.

They treated me _____ a child.

Lösungen

1. **by** taxi
   with a stone.
   with anything
   with his aunt
   at you
   with me
   by Stephen King
   with my wallet

2. **like** my brother
   as a bus driver
   like a hospital
   as a nurse
   like (such as) going
   like a professional
   such as paper
   like

Wortarten Seite 73

---

over, about, above   über,...

theme (Thema)   place (Ort)
Let's talk about music.   The picture is above the sofa.
A book about Religion.   Luise is climbing over the fence.

---

1 Fill in the correct prepositions. Use *about, over,* or *above*.

This exercise is _____ prepositions.

There are plenty of clouds _____ the trees.

Someone flew _____ the cuckoo's nest.

The Quarks live in the flat _____ ours.

The horse likes jumping _____ small rivers.

He told me _____ his adventures in the Himalaya.

We could talk to our children _____ a cup of tea.

High _____ the clouds freedom is beyond limits.

Tips & Hilfen:
Besonders wichtig ist es, sich die Präpositionen einzuprägen, bei denen die typischen Fehler passieren. Sie legen Übersetzungen nahe, die völlig in die Irre gehen.

mit dem Zug	by train	und nicht:	~~with the train~~
bei meiner Tante	with my aunt	und nicht:	~~by my aunt~~
von mir geschrieben	written by me	und nicht:	~~written from me~~
im Konzert	at the concert	und nicht:	~~in the concert~~
auf der Party	at the party	und nicht:	~~on the party~~
über der Tür	above the door	und nicht:	~~over the door~~
über dich reden	talk about you	und nicht:	~~talk over you~~

Lösungen

1. about prepositions
   above the trees
   over the cuckoo's nest
   above ours
   over small rivers
   about his adventures
   over a cup of tea
   above the clouds

Wortarten

Seite 74

> 💡 **Unbedingt merken:**
> Diese wichtigen Adjektive und Verben mit besonderen Präpositionen solltest du auswendig lernen.
>
> | | |
> |---|---|
> | to be afraid of s.th. / s.o. | – Angst haben vor etw. / jdm. |
> | to explain s.th. to s.o. | – jdm. etw. erklären |
> | to be angry with / at s.o. | – auf jdn. / mit jdm. böse sein |
> | to be different from s.th. / s.o. | – anders sein als etw. / jd. |
> | to laugh at s.o. | – jdn. auslachen |
> | to be delighted with s.th. | – über etw. erfreut sein |
> | to look at s.th. / s.o. | – etw. / jdn. anschauen |
> | to be good at s. th. | – gut sein in etw. |
> | to be mad about s.th. / s.o. | – verrückt sein nach etw. / jdm. |
> | to be mad at s.o. | – auf etw. / jdn. wütend sein |
> | to be interested in s.th. | – an etw. interessiert sein |
> | to remind s.o. of s.th. | – jdn. an etw. erinnern |
> | to be typical of s.th. / s.o. | – typisch sein für etw. / jdn. |
> | to believe in s.th. /s.o. | – an etw. / jdn. glauben |
> | to smile at s.o. | – jdn. anlächeln |
> | to dream of s.th. / s.o. | – von etw. / jdm. träumen |
> | to drive into s.th. / s.o. | – etw. / jdn. anfahren |
> | to wait for s.th. / s.o. | – auf jdn. / etw. warten |

1 Fill in the missing prepositions. Look them up in the list if you have to.

She had never been good _____ waiting. Suddenly she burst _____ tears. He had not arrived _____ the restaurant _____ the agreed time. She had always believed _____ him. Being late was not typical _____ him. "What's wrong _____ me?" she thought. She was really mad _____ him. He was so different _____ all the others. Whenever she looked _____ him, he reminded her _____ her father a little bit. How nicely he could smile _____ her! He had already kept her waiting _____ two hours. Wasn't he interested _____ her any more? Had he driven _____ a tree? Had a gangster shot _____ him? She was suffering _____ her own imagination. She was trembling _____ fear. And then she saw him getting _____ the bus just _____ the restaurant.

"I should be angry _____ him," she thought. "At least, he should explain _____ me why he was so late," she said _____ herself. But when he came _____ the room she just smiled _____ him. She was delighted _____ the sight _____ her boyfriend.

Lösungen

1. at waiting
   into tears
   at the restaurant
   at the agreed time
   in him
   of him
   with me
   about him
   from all the others
   at him
   of her
   at her
   for two hours
   in her
   into a tree
   at him
   from her own imagination
   with fear
   off the bus
   in front of the restaurant
   with him
   to me
   to herself
   into the room
   at him
   at the sight
   of her boyfriend

Wortarten

Conjunctions – Konjunktionen

> **Unbedingt merken:**
> Konjunktionen (Bindewörter) verbinden Satzglieder mit Satzgliedern und Sätze mit Sätzen. Besonders wichtig, weil für den Sinn des Satzgefüges entscheidend, sind die unterordnenden Konjunktionen, die Haupt- und Nebensätze (Gliedsätze) miteinander verbinden.
>
> boys and girls my mother or my father
> It is late and we are going home. I can walk or I can go by bike.
> When I was walking down the road, I noticed a man with a black beard.
> While I was walking down the road, I was looking at the shop windows.

Durch Konjunktionen werden folgende Beziehungen ausgedrückt:

Time (Zeit)

after	nachdem	till / until	bis
as	als, während	when	als, wenn
before	bevor	whenever	immer wenn
since	seit, seitdem	while	während

Cause (Grund)

as	da, weil	for	denn
because	da, weil	since	da (ja), weil

Andere wichtige Konjunktionen

(al)though	obwohl	that	daß
as	wie	where	wo
as if	als ob	wherever	wo(hin) auch immer
if	wenn, falls, ob	whether	ob
so (that)	so daß, damit	while	obwohl

> **Tips & Hilfen:**
> Groß ist die Verwechslungsgefahr zwischen *during* und *while*: *while* ist eine Konjunktion und leitet Nebensätze ein; *during* ist eine Präposition und steht vor Nomen.
> • Verwechsle auch nicht *when (als)* mit *while (während)*. Verwende *while* bei gleichzeitigen Vorgängen.

1 Add *when* or *while*.

_____ I was doing my homework, my sister was watching TV.

I was talking to my business partner _____ George arrived.

_____ the doorbell rang, I was sitting at my desk.

John was fighting the gangsters _____ I was calling the police.

Jerry was biting his nails _____ Tom was driving his car.

Lösungen

1. While I was doing my homework …
   … when George arrived.
   When the doorbell rang …
   … while I was calling the police.
   … while Tom was driving his car.

Seite 76 — Wortarten

> **Tips & Hilfen:**
> Ein typischer Fehler besteht darin, die Konjunktion *as* in Adverbialsätzen des Grundes mit *als* zu übersetzen. *As* heißt hier *weil*, *da* und kann durch *since* ersetzt werden:
> *As / Since we live near the sea, we often go sailing.*

1 Translate the following sentences.

Da die Bakers in meiner Nähe wohnen, sehe ich sie oft.

_____

Weil wir das Auto nicht sehr oft benötigen, werden wir es verkaufen.

_____

Weil ich müde war, ging ich früh zu Bett.

_____

> **Tips & Hilfen:**
> Benutze *because* nicht am Satzanfang. Verwende statt dessen *as* oder *since*.
>
> Ursache ➜ Folge   Folge ⬅ Ursache
> so – so daß   because – weil
>
> *I took no notice of him so he flew into a rage.*
> *He flew into a rage because I took no notice of him.*

2 Change the sentences. Use *so* or *because*.

I'll take the train _____ I won't get stuck in a traffic jam.

My classmates like me _____ I'm not arrogant.

I'm leaving home _____ I'm fed up with my family.

I sent my kids away _____ I could invite all my friends.

We'll write him some friendly words _____ he's happy again.

I don't want to go home _____ it's so nice at school.

3 Join the sentences using *either – or*.

You leave the office. I'll call the police.

_____

You can have bananas. You can have plums. You can have pears.

_____

You can come with me. You can also go home.

_____

Lösungen

1. As / Since the Bakers live near me, I often see them.
   As / Since we don't need the car very often, we'll sell it.
   As / Since I was tired, I went to bed early.

2. so
   because
   because
   so
   so
   because

3. Either you leave the office or I'll call the police.
   You can have either bananas, plums or pears.
   You can either come with me or go home.

Wortarten

Seite 77

1 Join the sentences with *not only ... but also*.

Tom was late. He was also noisy.

Tom was not only late but also noisy.

She's an excellent housewife. She is also a first-class musician.

She _____ but _____

She sings like an angel. She also dances like a ballet-dancer.

She _____ but _____

Tips & Hilfen:

whereas drückt einen Gegensatz zwischen Dingen/Personen aus und kann durch *while* ersetzt werden.

However verwendet man bei einem sehr pointierten Gegensatz:

Yvonne is very intelligent whereas her brother is rather stupid.
Yvonne is very intelligent. However, her brother is rather stupid.

---

2 Join the sentences by using *whereas* where possible. Otherwise use *however*.

The weather at the sea was horrible. The children enjoyed it.

The weather _____

Diana was very talkative. Her sister was very quiet.

Diana _____

I like the sea. You prefer the mountains.

I _____

He was extremely tired. He was unable to sleep on the plane.

He _____

My friend Harry drinks too much. My friend Colin eats too much.

My friend _____

Your brother works hard. You are lazy.

Your _____

Lösungen

1. She's not only an excellent housewife but also a first-class musician.
   She not only sings like an angel but also dances like a ballet-dancer.

2. However
   whereas
   whereas
   However
   whereas
   whereas

Wortarten

Unbedingt merken:
Gegensätze werden durch *though* oder *although* (obgleich, obwohl) ausgedrückt. Wenn eine Bedingung daran geknüpft ist, benutzt man *even if (selbst wenn):*
Although he had worked hard for many weeks, he didn't look tired.
Even if I win the lottery I'll not buy a Porsche as my second car.
Bei Vergleichssätzen verwendet man die Konjunktion *as (wie);* wenn eine Bedingung damit verknüpft ist, heißt es *as if (als ob).*
They did as they promised.
You look as if you've seen a ghost.

1 Join the sentences. Use *(al)though* or *even if.*

The noise kept him awake. He was very tired.
The noise kept him awake although he was very tired.

I always enjoy sailing. / ? / The weather is very rough.
_____

He wouldn't give me the money. / ? / I begged him.
_____

We'll go to the zoo. / ? / The weather is bad.
_____

He looked strong and healthy. / ? / He hadn't eaten anything.
_____

People always want more money. / ? / They are rich.
_____

2 Insert *as* or *as if.*

Look! You should have done it _____ I showed you.

It looks _____ it's going to rain.

_____ you know, it's Lucy's birthday next week.

It looks _____ all children like spaghetti with tomato sauce.

Tips & Hilfen:
Die Konjunktion *as* kann nicht einfach anstelle von *like (wie)* verwendet werden, auch wenn das in der Umgangssprache gebräuchlich ist:
Why didn't you write to me like Susan?
Why didn't you write to me as (you have) promised?
He moved like a road runner.
He moved as if he had never broken his leg.

Lösungen

1. The noise kept him awake although he was very tired.
   I always enjoy sailing even if the weather is very rough.
   He wouldn't give me the money although I begged him.
   We'll go to the zoo even if the weather is bad.
   He looked strong and healthy although he hadn't eaten anything.
   People always want more money even if they are rich.

2. … as I showed you
   … as if it's going to rain
   As you know …
   It looks as if …

Kapitel 5

Arbeit mit Texten

Textarbeit besteht immer aus zwei großen Bereichen: Zum einen geht es um das Verständnis eines vorgegebenen Textes, zum anderen um das Verfassen eigener Texte auf der Grundlage dieses Verständnisses.

Gutes Textverständnis ist Voraussetzung jeder Textarbeit:
Du kannst davon ausgehen, daß alle Aufgaben, die zu einem Text gestellt werden, ausschließlich dazu dienen, dir das Textverständnis zu erleichtern: Bei Comprehension-Fragen (Verständnisfragen) wird direkt auf den Text Bezug genommen. Sie prüfen nicht nur, ob du den Text verstanden hast, sie geben dir zugleich Hilfestellung. In der Regel sind diese Fragen streng am Ablauf der Texte orientiert. Auch die Aufgaben zu Wortschatz und Grammatik sind direkt auf das vorliegende Textmaterial bezogen und dienen dem besseren Textverständnis.

Unbedingt merken:

Du solltest dir stets ausreichend Zeit für die Textlektüre nehmen: Mache dabei nicht den Fehler und versuche, den Text gleich ins Deutsche zu übertragen.

- Das erste Lesen dient ausschließlich dem groben Erfassen des Inhalts. Einzelheiten sind an dieser Stelle nicht ausschlaggebend. Auch unbekannte Wörter und Ausdrücke kannst du zunächst getrost überlesen. Lies den Text bis zum Ende durch, und mache dir klar, worum es geht, was die Grundaussage oder der wesentliche Handlungsstrang ist. Was ist dein erster Eindruck?
- Erst bei der zweiten Lektüre nimmst du Stift oder Textmarker zur Hand. Hebe die Textstellen hervor, die dir für den Aufbau der Handlung oder Argumentation bedeutsam erscheinen. Nun kannst du versuchen, das, was du beim ersten Lesen nicht verstanden hast, aus der Kenntnis des Gesamtzusammenhangs zu erschließen.
- Wenn jetzt noch Fragen offen sind, solltest du ein Wörterbuch zu Rate ziehen. Schlage nur die Vokabeln nach, die für das Textverständnis insgesamt unbedingt notwendig sind.

1 Was wird deiner Meinung nach beim Verfassen eines Textes von dir erwartet?

Tips & Hilfen:

Zur Beantwortung gestellter Fragen mußt du dich genau an den vorgegebenen Text und seinen Aufbau halten. Häufig kannst du Formulierungen und Wendungen des Textes aufgreifen und für deine Antwort verwenden. Einfach abschreiben allerdings solltest du nicht; besonders über die korrekte Zeitform mußt du dir Gedanken machen.

Lösungen

1. Der eigene Text soll zeigen, daß du in der Lage bist, selbständig Gedanken in der Fremdsprache zu formulieren. Ganz wichtig ist dafür, daß du den vorgegebenen Text verstanden hast.

Teenage Tragedy

Yesterday fifteen-year-old Hanan S. was found in her room. An overdose of sleeping pills seems to have been the cause of death. As no external injuries were found, the police came to the conclusion that she committed suicide. If this is true, Hanan is the 36th victim of teenage suicide in the Greater London area this year.

Hanan's family lives in St John's Wood. Her father, Muhammad S., aged 42, has been working as a bus conductor since he left Pakistan and came to Britain in 1978. Hanan lived with her parents and her two sisters on a council estate mainly inhabited by immigrants from Pakistan, India and Bangladesh.

Hanan was born in England and went to Montgomery Comprehensive School. Her teachers and classmates describe her as having been lively and open-minded. Her interests included dancing, music and sports (she enjoyed watching tennis on TV and played in the school's hockey team). She was popular with the girls in her class, but didn't have a boyfriend. Until last November, that is.

Things changed when she met Brian J., a 16-year-old boy at her school and captain of the rugby team. She was fascinated by his fair hair, his blue eyes and his physical strength. At first Brian wasn't aware of Hanan's attention, but this changed with the help from her friends. He asked her out for a drink after school. They found they had a lot in common and Brian invited her to go with him to the local disco the following Friday.

She had never been to a disco before and as a girl who respected and trusted her parents it was the obvious thing to ask her parents' permission. Hanan's father didn't like the idea of his daughter going to discotheques, and when he learned that Brian was neither Muslim nor from Pakistan, he refused to let her go.

Although living in Britain since 1978, Mr S. is still deeply rooted in Pakistani traditions and has always tried to raise his children in the same way his parents had raised him. He accepts western culture and its advantages, but nevertheless expects his family to live a life according to Asian values. He is against girls having the right to choose their own way of life.

Hanan had never contradicted her father, but on this occasion decided to fight his decision. After a number of heated discussions that involved the whole family, Mr S. threatened to send his daughter back to her grandparents in Pakistan.

Hanan knew other girls who had been sent to Pakistan – a country they had never lived in – and were forced to marry a complete stranger. This would be the end of a life she had got used to and the end of her dreams for the future.

Hanan's youngest sister discovered her body. Hanan S. – a victim of two cultures?

Arbeit mit Texten

Seite 81

1 Answer in complete sentences.

a) What does the text tell you about Hanan?
   (age, looks, character, interests, …)

b) What do you learn about her father?
   (age, occupation, religion, ideals, …)

c) How did Hanan feel about her parents?
   (respect, trust …)

d) What did Hanan and Brian plan to do?

e) How did her father react when she told him about her plans? What reasons did he give?

f) What did he threaten to do if Hanan didn't listen to him?

g) Why didn't she want to go back to Pakistan?

Tips & Hilfen:
Zur Beantwortung der Fragen kannst du auf Redewendungen zurückgreifen, die in den Fragestellungen auftauchen. Benutze die dort gebrauchten Zeitformen. Verwende möglichst einfache und kurze Sätze.

Lösungen

1. a) Hanan was a fifteen-year-old girl interested in dancing, music and sports. She was lively, open-minded and popular with the girls in her class.
b) Hanan's father, Muhammad S., is 42 and works as a bus conductor. He is a Muslim who accepts western culture. But he expects his family to live a life according to Asian values.
c) Hanan respected and trusted her parents. She never contradicted her father.
d) They wanted to go to the local disco.
e) Mr S. didn't want his daughter to go to a disco with Brian because Brian is not a Muslim or a Pakistani. He wants his daughter to live according to Pakistani traditions. He doesn't think girls have the right to choose their own way of life.
f) Mr S. threatened to send Hanan back to her grandparents in Pakistan.
g) Hanan didn't want to go back to Pakistan because she knew other girls who had been sent there and were forced to marry a complete stranger. This would be the end of the life she had got used to and the end of her dreams for the future.

Seite 82   *Arbeit mit Texten*

1 Explain the following expressions from the text in your own words. Write complete sentences.

… an overdose of sleeping pills … *(lines 2/3)*

She took so many sleeping pills that she died.

… she was popular with the girls … *(line 13)*

… he is deeply rooted in Pakistani traditions … *(line 25)*

… western culture and its advantages *(line 27)*

… choose their own way of life … *(lines 28/29)*

… to fight his decision … *(lines 30/31)*

Tips & Hilfen:

Manchmal werden gegenteilige Bedeutungen mit Hilfe von Vorsilben *(prefixes)* ausgedrückt:

dis-:	to approve – to **dis**approve	il-:	legal – **il**legal
in-:	secure – **in**secure	im-:	mature – **im**mature
non-:	member – **non**-member	un-:	successful – **un**successful

Diese Vorsilben müssen jeweils angefügt bzw. weggelassen werden.

---

2 Find the opposites.

to agree	– to disagree	known	–
emigrant	–	respect	–
interested	–	to distrust	–
unpopular	–	to dislike	–
unaware	–	disadvantage	–
inattention	–	to complete	–

3 Find synonyms (words with the same meaning) in the text.

to appear	–	commander	–
evident	–	consent	–
however	–	to include	–

Lösungen

1. The girls liked her (very much).
   Pakistani traditions are very important to Mr S. / His beliefs are based on Pakistani traditions. / He believes in Pakistani traditions.
   the western world / western values / western way of life and the opportunity to work and earn money.
   Western culture made it possible to live their lives the way they want.
   to fight for her point of view / not to give in to other people / to oppose his decision / to fight for her point of view

2. to disagree   unknown
   immigrant   disrespect
   disinterested   to trust
   popular   to like
   aware   advantage
   attention   to incomplete

3. to seem   captain
   (line 3)   *(line 15)*
   obvious   permission
   (line 22)   *(line 22)*
   nevertheless   involve
   (line 27)   *(line 31)*

Arbeit mit Texten   **Seite 83**

Tips & Hilfen:
Ganz wichtig für jede Textarbeit sind die *question words*, mit denen Fragen an den Text gestellt werden können:

who?	persons	wer? wen? wem?
what?	things, facts or events	was? was für (ein)?
which?	persons or things	welche/r/s aus einer Menge?
whose?	owners	wessen?
when?	time and duration	wann?
where?	place and direction	wo? wohin?
why?	reason	warum?
how?	way or method	wie?

Nicht verwechseln:
whose? = wessen? – who's? = who is?
who? = wer? – where? = wo?

Unbedingt merken:
Wenn im Aussagesatz kein Hilfsverb steht, muß die Frage mit *to do* umschrieben werden, damit die regelmäßige Wortstellung *Subjekt – Prädikat – Objekt* erhalten bleibt.
They came from Pakistan – Where did they come from?

1 Form questions to which the given statements are the answers.

Hanan's family lives in <u>St. John's Wood</u>

Where does Hanan's family live?

Mr S. came to Britain in <u>1978</u>.

Hanan went to <u>Montgomery Comprehensive School.</u>

Brain's eyes are <u>blue</u>.

Brian invited Hanan to <u>the local disco</u>.

Hanan's father came to Britain <u>in 1978</u>.

Hanan's body was discovered by <u>her little sister</u>.

Lösungen

1. When did Mr. S. come to Britain?
   Which school did Hanan go to?
   What colour are Brian's eyes?
   Which disco did Brian invite Hanan to? / What did Brian invite Hanan to?
   When did Hanan's father come to Britain?
   Who was Hanan found by?

Seite 84

Arbeit mit Texten

Unbedingt merken:
Ein *comment* ist eine persönliche Stellungnahme zu einer vorgegebenen Aussage. Der *comment* steht in engem Zusammenhang mit der Textvorlage.

Tips & Hilfen:
Halte zunächst deine Gedanken in Form von Stichworten fest. Bringe sie dann in eine sinnvolle Reihenfolge: Stelle die weniger wichtigen an den Anfang und die wichtigsten an den Schluß.
In einem einleitenden Satz formulierst du das Problem. Dabei greifst du die Fragestellung auf.

Dann legst du deine Ansicht dar.
I think (that) …, I believe (that) …, I am of the opinion …, In my opinion …, I am convinced (that) …, My personal point of view is (that) …

Damit der Leser deine Ansicht nachvollziehen und sich möglicherweise überzeugen lassen kann, sollte sie durch Argumente gestützt sein.
I believe (this) because …, because of …, The reason for … is …, My opinion / statement is based on / backed by …, In my experience …

Ergänze deine Argumente um Beispiele oder Gegenbeispiele.
This can be illustrated by …, An example for this is …, This is shown by …, To give an example (of) …, This demonstrates …, It shows …, It proves …, for example …, for instance …, To illustrate this …,

Abschließend faßt du deine Ansicht in einem Schlußsatz zusammen.

1 Hanan could have chosen the easy way out and not have asked her father's permission at all. What do you think? Give reasons.

Lösungen

1. For example:
I think Hanan had no other choice than to ask her father's permission to go out with Brian. She talked to her father because she trusted and respected him. There was no easy way out for Hanan. She knew she had to fight her father's decision. But she should have asked her friends for help.

Arbeit mit Texten

Seite 85

1 Do you think that children should have the right to choose their own way of life? Explain your point of view.

2 Hanan killed herself out of desperation. If she had been your friend, what advice would you have given her?

Tips & Hilfen:
Lies deinen Text zum Schluß mindestens einmal gründlich durch – nicht nur um mögliche Fehler zu korrigieren, sondern auch um zu überprüfen,
- ob er klar und verständlich formuliert ist,
- ob er den Leser überzeugen kann,
- ob er in sich logisch und konsequent aufgebaut ist.

Lösungen

1. For example:
   I believe that – to a certain extent – all children should have the right to choose the way they want to live when they are as old as Brian and Hanan. They have to decide on quite a lot of things on their own, anyway. But there are other things which parents are responsible for and which they should discuss with their children. Not all children, for example, are fond of going to school day by day. If they could do what they wanted, only teachers would go to school.

2. For example:
   As her friend, I would have told Hanan that she should have talked to other people about her problems. She could have asked one of our teachers to talk to her parents. Perhaps Hanan's father would have listened to the arguments of another grown-up and the tragedy could have been avoided.

Dian Fossey

Dian Fossey was about thirty years old when she first travelled to Africa in 1963. On her travels in Africa she met Louis Leakey, a famous scientist. Under his influence she decided to devote herself to the protection of mountain gorillas – an exceptionally rare and endangered species.

At that time, only a few hundred of these animals lived high up in the mountain region, deep in the heart of Central Africa on the borders of Rwanda, Uganda and Zaire. As the human population is increasing and the need for food and farming land is constantly growing, the habitat of wild animals is becoming smaller and smaller. Having no enemies but men, the gorillas were forced higher and higher up the misty mountains. Although they were strictly protected by law, they were not safe from being hunted even here. Illegal hunters chased and killed them wherever they could and threatened their survival.

Dian Fossey gave up her job, left her family and friends in America and established a small research station up in the Virunga Mountains. She lived in the wilderness for 18 years, all alone in a small lodge. She was convinced that you have to know and study the animals you want to protect. So she began to observe man's closest relatives, their social behaviour and the way they live and feed themselves.

Her dream came true when she saw a group of gorillas for the first time. As gorillas are extremely shy and nervous, they quickly disappeared back into the jungle. As time went by, Dian Fossey became more familiar with these shy giants. She was able to distinguish one gorilla from another. She called them Petula, Bartok and Uncle Bert. However, she knew that she was only being tolerated by the gorillas. After a year or so she watched a young gorilla eating leaves and roots. He suddenly put down his food, turned around and stared at her. When their eyes met, Dian Fossey knew that the barrier between man and animal had been breached for a brief moment.

By imitating the gorillas' gestures and noises, she managed to build up a good relationship with them. The gorillas were not dangerous and terrifying at all. They lived together peacefully and amicably. Two years later, Dian Fossey was an accepted member of the gorilla community. No wonder that she was fascinated by their harmonious way of life. If only man could learn to live together so peacefully as these animals, she thought.

However, one day this peace was shattered. One misty morning she discovered the dead body of Digit, a male gorilla, that had become her special friend. His head and hands had been cut off as trophies. Over the past twenty years nearly half of the gorilla population has been wiped out by illegal hunters. Dian Fossey suspected that National Park gamekeepers were involved in these killings. She therefore established the "Digit Foundation" with the aim of protecting the gorillas against illegal hunters. By doing this she incurred their bitter hatred.

At Christmas 1985 she was found in her lodge with her head split open. She was probably murdered by these hunters, but the truth has never been established.

Arbeit mit Texten

Seite 87

1 Read the text thoroughly – at least twice. Then try to answer the following questions in complete sentences. Only state the main points.

1 Why did Dian Fossey go to Africa?

2 What are the wild living mountain gorillas threatened by?

3 How did Dian Fossey want to help the gorillas?

4 What aspects fascinated Dian Fossey in particular?

5 What do we learn about Digit?

6 Why did people hate and finally kill Dian Fossey?

Lösungen

1. **1** Influenced by Louis Leakey, a famous scientist, Dian Fossey wanted to protect the wild mountain gorillas. It was her dream to help these animals. *(lines 2–5)*

   2 Humans are the only enemies of the wild mountain gorillas. The gorillas are threatened by farmers who need more land for farming to feed the growing population. But their worst enemies are illegal hunters, who kill the gorillas wherever they can. *(lines 8–13)*

   3 Dian Fossey thought the best way for a scientist to help endangered animals was to observe their social behaviour and the way they live and feed themselves. *(lines 16–18)*

   4 Dian Fossey was particularly fascinated by the harmonious, peaceful and amicable way the animals live together. *(lines 29–33)*

   5 The gorilla called Digit became Dian Fossey's special friend. He was killed by illegal hunters who cut off his head and hands as hunting trophies. *(lines 34–36)*

   6 Dian Fossey had established the "Digit Foundation" which intended to protect the wild mountain gorillas against illegal hunting. That was why they hated and finally murdered her. *(lines 37–40)*

Seite 88   *Arbeit mit Texten*

> **Tips & Hilfen:**
> Wenn du eine Vokabel nicht kennst, suche zuerst nach bekannten Wortbestandteilen (z. B. *wilderness*) oder nach Entsprechungen in der deutschen oder englischen Sprache (z. B. *giant – Gigant, gigantisch*).

1 Explain the following words used in the text – if necessary with the help of your dictionary.

… scientist … *(line 3)*

A scientist is a person with a special knowledge in certain disciplines for example in chemistry or mathematics.

… endangered species … *(line 5)*

… habitat of wild animals … *(line 9)*

… barrier between man and animal … *(line 26)*

… good relationship … *(lines 28/29)*

… shattered peace… *(line 34)*

… the aim of protecting … *(line 39)*

2 Find one expression for the followings word groups. Mind the plural!

Petula, Bartok and Uncle Bert are

Chimpanzees, orang-utans and gorillas are

Huts, lodges and cabins are

Rwanda, Uganda and Zaire are

3 Find a word in the text with the same meaning.

to give all your energy to something

extraordinarily

in a friendly way

guard of a National Park

Lösungen

1. Endangered species are animals like the mountain gorillas in Africa which are not able to survive without protection.
   A habitat of wild animals is the natural environment where wild animals live and are not disturbed by people.
   A barrier between men and animals is a border which separates man from animals.
   People or animals who like each other and take care of each other have a good relationship.
   A shattered peace is a peace which is disturbed and has been broken.
   The aim of protecting means the plan to take care and safeguard someone or something against harm or danger.

2. Petula, Bartok and Uncle Bert are gorillas / monkeys / apes / animals.
   Chimpanzees, orang-utans and gorillas are animals / monkeys / apes.
   Huts, lodges and cabins are houses.
   Rwanda, Uganda and Zaire are countries (in Central Africa).

3. to devote oneself *(line 4)*
   exceptionally *(line 4)*
   amicably *(line 30)*
   gamekeeper *(line 38)*

Arbeit mit Texten **Seite 89**

1 Form active into passive sentences.

Illegal hunters chase and kill the mountain gorillas.

The mountain gorillas are

At first the gorillas only tolerated the scientist.

Then they accepted her.

Someone killed Dian Fossey.

Unbedingt merken:
Texte sind in Absätze untergliedert; das gibt dir wichtige Hinweise für die Gliederung. Wenn du jedem Absatz eine Überschrift zuordnest, also den Inhalt in einem knappen Satz klar und verständlich wiedergibst, hast du im Kern schon so etwas wie die Inhaltsangabe eines Textes geleistet. Denn so wird Absatz für Absatz das Wesentliche vom Unwesentlichen getrennt.

Tips & Hilfen:
Die folgenden Wendungen sind für das Verfassen von Gliederungen und Inhaltsangaben sehr nützlich. Am besten prägst du sie dir gut ein. Du wirst sie immer wieder gebrauchen können.

The paragraph is about …	Der Abschnitt handelt von …
The paragraph deals with …	Der Abschnitt beschäftigt sich mit …
The subject of the story is …	Das Thema der Geschichte ist …
The text presents …	Der Text stellt … vor.
The general idea of the text …	Der Hauptgedanke des Textes …
The problem of … is discussed	Das Problem … wird erörtert

2 The text "Dian Fossey" is divided into seven paragraphs. What is each paragraph about? Read the text again. Then write one sentence which describes the content of each paragraph.

The first paragraph introduces Dian Fossey and her idea of protecting the mountain gorillas. The second paragraph

---

Lösungen

1. The mountain gorillas are chased and killed by illegal hunters. At first the scientist was only tolerated by the gorillas. Then she was accepted. Dian Fossey was killed.

2. The second paragraph describes the living conditions of the gorillas.
   The third paragraph is about the research station which Dian Fossey established to observe the primates.
   The fourth paragraph describes how Dian Fossey came into contact with the gorillas.
   The fifth paragraph tells us how fascinated Dian Fossey was by living with gorillas.
   The subject of the sixth paragraph is the killing of Digit, a gorilla who became Dian Fossey's special friend, and the establishment of a foundation for the protection of mountain gorillas.
   In the final paragraph we learn that Dian Fossey herself was murdered for her activities on behalf of the gorillas.

Arbeit mit Texten

1 Now find a title for the story summarising the content.

> **Tips & Hilfen:**
> Nicht immer macht ein Titel deutlich, worum es im Text geht, was sein Thema ist. Wenn es dir gelingt, nichtssagende Überschriften durch aussagekräftige zu ersetzen, dann hast du den Inhalt eines Textes gleichsam auf den Begriff gebracht. Und du zeigst, daß du sein Thema erfaßt hast.

2 Write a report on Dian Fossey's life for the local newspaper "The Karisoke Jungle Post".

> **Unbedingt merken:**
> Ein Bericht *(report)* soll sich auf das Wesentliche beschränken und deshalb knapp und präzise die Umstände eines Geschehens wiedergeben. Dabei sollen nach Möglichkeit folgende Fragen beantwortet werden:
> - Wann und an welchem Ort fand das Geschehen statt?
> - Gibt es ein Vorgeschehen? – Achte auf die zeitliche Abfolge.
> - Welche Personen sind beteiligt?
> - Wie läßt sich die Hauptperson kurz charakterisieren?
> - Welche Folgen haben die Ereignisse für die Zukunft?
>
> Achte besonders auf die Formulierung des Einleitungssatzes. Er muß bereits deutlich machen, worum es geht.

Lösungen

1. For example:
   Life with the gorillas /
   A life for the gorillas

2. For example:
   At Christmas 1985, Dian Fossey, the famous researcher, was found dead in her lodge. It is suspected that she was murdered by illegal hunters of the mountain gorillas she was protecting. Dian Fossey came to Africa in 1963 and devoted her life to the protection of the mountain gorillas. She left her country, her friends and her job to study the gorillas in their natural habitat. For this purpose she founded a small research station in the Virunga Mountains where she lived for 18 years. She also established the "Digit Foundation" to protect the animals against illegal hunting. She will always be remembered as a great scientist who lost her life in her fight for the survival of the endangered species of the mountain gorillas.

Arbeit mit Texten

During the course of evolution (the development of life on our planet) most plants and animals have died out. The dinosaurs are only the best known example. Nowadays every few seconds another species becomes extinct. Should we take action to stop this?
Think of the costs, the constantly growing population and its expanding need for resources (food, clothing, farming land etc.).

1 What's your opinion? Give reasons and examples. Write a comment of about 100–120 words.

Lösungen

1. For example:
   During the course of evolution, plants and animals have developed and become extinct. But today the survival of all species has become important. If you take other developments like global warming or nuclear energy into account, then it's high time to do something about it. I think it is not pure chance that people in highly industrialised countries take special care of the protection of endangered species, whereas people of the poorer countries in the Third World with their steadily growing population have to struggle for their own survival. If we don't do anything about the increasing consumption of resources everywhere – particularly to cover the needs of the people in industrial countries – it might be too late not only for some species but also for the survival of mankind.

A letter to the editor

Dear Sir,

I'm afraid I do not understand my son any more. Ian is fifteen and has completely changed over the last year. He used to go out and play every day. He never wanted to stay at home. Now he spends all his spare time in his room with his computer.

It all started about a year ago when I bought him a computer. Although I do not know anything about computers, I thought it would be a good idea for him to learn to use one. After all, the media are always telling us about the blessings of this new technology. It is said to bring about a radical change in cultural technology, which can only be compared to the invention of the wheel. Those who do not learn to work with computers are not fit for tomorrow's world, they say. Of course I do not wish my son to be a digital dunce and it was for this reason that I decided to buy him a computer. My intention was to prepare him for the future.

Much to my surprise, he sat down at the computer and patiently began to struggle with bits and bytes. I thought the initial fascination would wear off and he would get down to some sensible work on the computer. I bought all kinds of tutorial software for English, Maths and Geography. Ian was enthusiastic, but his school marks did not get any better. On the contrary, they got worse!

It is bad enough that Ian's school reports are getting worse, but losing interest in everything else and isolating himself in his room is even worse. He does not go to soccer training sessions any more and has not been to the Scouts for ages. His friends visit him less and less. For a while they came round to pick him up so that they could go out to do sports.

When I try to get him away from the computer, all he says is, "You don't understand!" He explains that a computer has its own logic which is clear and straightforward. "There is only right or wrong. That is what is fascinating and not ball games." Now he has gone completely mad. He wants to write his own programs …

I do not know what to do any more. How does one cope with a son who is obsessed by computers and whose mind has gone digital? Can you give me any advice?

Yours sincerely,
Elaine Kendall

Arbeit mit Texten

Seite 93

1 Read the letter and answer the questions.

Why did Mrs Kendall write her letter?
_____
_____
_____

What happened to Ian?
_____
_____
_____
_____

What does the media say about computers?
_____
_____

Why did Mrs Kendall buy a computer for her son?
_____
_____

What were the consequences for Ian's performance at school?
_____
_____

What further consequences is Mrs Kendall complaining about?
_____
_____
_____
_____

2 Find words in the text with the same meaning.

plan   _____
to fight   _____
attraction   _____
program   _____
meetings   _____

Lösungen

1. Mrs Kendall wrote her letter to the editor because she didn't understand her son Ian any more / because she had a problem with her son Ian. Ian has changed since his mother bought him a computer.
He doesn't go out any more and spends all his time at the computer instead. The media say that computers are to bring about a radical change in cultural technology, which can only be compared to the invention of the wheel.
Mrs Kendall did not want her son to be a digital dunce. She wanted to prepare him for the future.
Ian's marks did not get better. They got worse.
She is complaining about Ian isolating himself. He does not go to soccer training sessions anymore and has not been to the Scouts for ages. His friends visit him less and less.

2. intention *(line 13)*
   to struggle *(line 14)*
   fascination *(line 15)*
   software *(line 16)*
   sessions *(line 21)*

Seite 94

Arbeit mit Texten

1 Explain the meaning of the following expressions in your own words.

A letter to the editor is _____

An invention is _____

2 Find three words that belong to one of the following groups.

Editor, teacher, and carpenter are occupations.

_____ are media.

_____ are cultural technologies.

_____ are school subjects.

3 Which expression does not belong to each group? Give a reason.

bits and bytes, invention, software

_____

marks, reports, forms, Scouts

_____

> **Unbedingt merken:**
>
> *Question tags* sind Frageanhängsel, die ein Sprecher verwendet, wenn er eine Bestätigung erwartet. Ist die Aussage des Satzes bejaht, so wird der *question tag* verneint. Ist sie verneint, so wird der *question tag* bejaht.
>
> Jan likes computers, doesn't he?
> Mrs Kendall doesn't like computers, does she?

4 Form questions by adding question tags.

Mrs Kendall doesn't understand her son anymore, _____?

The media always talk about computer technology, _____?

Jan's school reports are getting worse and worse, _____?

He does not go to football training sessions anymore, _____?

He has gone completely mad, _____?

The logic of a computer is fascinating, _____?

Lösungen

1. A letter to the editor is a letter addressed to a newspaper *(heading)*
   An invention is something created for the first time. *(line 10)*

2. Television, newspapers and radio are media.
   Reading, writing and calculating are cultural technologies.
   English, Maths and Geography are school subjects.

3. Bits and bytes and software are things which have to do with computers. An invention is something created new.
   Marks, reports, and forms are something to do with school. The scouts are an organization for boys.

4. does she?
   don't they?
   aren't they?
   does he?
   hasn't he?
   isn't it?

Arbeit mit Texten

Seite 95

Tips & Hilfen:
Bei der Wiedergabe von wörtlicher Rede braucht man die indirekte Rede (reported speech). Beachte die richtige Wortstellung, die entsprechenden Personalpronomen und die Zeitenfolge.

1 Rewrite the dialogue in reported speech.

Mrs Kendall: "Why don't you stop playing with that computer. And why don't you go to the Scouts?"
Ian: "You don't understand anything! I'm not playing at all."
Mrs Kendall: "But you have never been to the Boy Scouts ever since you got the computer."
Ian: "They only play foolish games and do nothing but waste time."
Mrs Kendall: "You couldn't get enough of those games in the past."
Ian: "And now I do things which make sense."
Mrs Kendall: "What fascinates you so much about computers?"
Ian: "Computers don't ask silly questions."

Mrs Kendall asked her son Jan

2 In her letter Mrs Kendall quotes what the media say and what her son thinks about computers. Underline the arguments which support the use of computers and form sentences with these arguments.

Lösungen

1. Mrs Kendall asked her son Ian why he didn't stop playing with the computer, and why he didn't go to the Scouts. Ian answered that she didn't understand anything, and said (that) he was not playing at all.
Mrs Kendall pointed out that he had never been to the Boy Scouts ever since he had got the computer.
Ian replied that they only played foolish games, and did nothing but waste time.
Mrs Kendall reminded him that he couldn't get enough of those games in the past.
Ian answered her that he now did things which make sense.
Mrs Kendall asked what fascinated him so much about computers.
Ian replied that computers didn't (don't) ask silly questions.

2. The arguments:
change in cultural technology *(line 9),* fit for tomorrow's world *(line 11),* all kinds of tutorial software *(line 16),* clear and straightforward logic *(lines 25/26),* own programs *(line 27)*
Computers are a new cultural technology. To be fit for tomorrow's world we have to learn how to work with them. There are all kinds of software. For examples, pupils can use tutorial software to learn for English, Maths and other school subjects. The logic of computers is clear and straightforward, and if you are really fit you can write your own programs for your individual purpose.

Arbeit mit Texten

> **Unbedingt merken:**
> Ein *personal comment* bezieht sich immer auf Aussagen und Argumente des Textes: Welche Fragen werden dort aufgeworfen, welche Themen angesprochen? Was ist das zentrale Problem? Drücke deine Zustimmung oder Ablehnung aus, führe Gründe an und unterbreite Vorschläge.

1 Answer the letter to the editor. Give Mrs Kendall some advice (about 100 words).

Lösungen

1. For example:
   Dear Mrs Kendall,
   In your letter you say that you don't understand your son any more. He spends all his spare time with the computer struggling with bits and bytes. You also write that his marks at school are getting worse and worse and that he is no longer interested in sports and other things.
   Of course, you can't let Ian go on like this. But you should also take him seriously. You should tell him that he can use the computer only at certain times, for example, in the evening till 10 o'clock or at the weekends. He can also do his homework on it or try to write programs. It may be useful for the future.
   You'll see that your son …

   Yours sincerely,